Solieman Abdul Jafar

READINGS FROM THE MYSTICS OF ISLĀM

KARMA - the ups, down,
vigil dexterity of life.

READINGS
FROM THE
MYSTICS OF ISLĀM

TRANSLATIONS FROM THE ARABIC AND PERSIAN, TOGETHER WITH A SHORT ACCOUNT OF THE HISTORY AND DOCTRINES OF ṢŪFISM AND BRIEF BIOGRAPHICAL NOTES ON EACH ṢŪFĪ WRITER

By

MARGARET SMITH, M.A. D.Lit.

LONDON
LUZAC & COMPANY LTD.,
46 GREAT RUSSELL STREET, W.C. 1
1972

First published	1950
Reprinted	1972

SBN 7189 01622

Printed in Great Britain
by Stephen Austin and Sons Ltd., Hertford

ALPHABETICAL LIST OF AUTHORS

PREFACE

This book, containing a short account of the history and development of Islamic mysticism, followed by translations of the sayings and writings of nearly fifty of the mystics of Islam, both Arab and Persian, may be a means of increasing the reader's knowledge of Islamic mysticism and interest in it. The passages chosen cover a period of over a thousand years, from the 8th to the middle of the 19th century A.D. They are arranged in chronological order and each is prefixed by a few lines giving biographical details of the mystic concerned, though of a few of them practically nothing is known.

Some of these translations have appeared before and I have to thank the Syndics of the Cambridge University Press, the Sheldon Press, and Mr. John Murray, for permission to reprint them.

The book includes an appendix supplying references to the Arabic and Persian texts from which the translations were made.

MARGARET SMITH

May, 1950.

ṢŪFISM,

A BRIEF ACCOUNT OF THE MYSTICISM FOUND IN ISLĀM

MYSTICISM is to be found as a vital element in many religious faiths and especially in the early religions of the East, in the Vedic literature, in the Buddhism of India and China, in Judaism, in Greece, in Christianity, and also in Islām, where it established itself at an early date and made itself felt in all Islamic countries, especially Egypt, Persia, Turkey and India.

This mysticism had its rise in a revolt of the soul, in those who were really spiritually minded, against formality in religion and also against indifference to religion, and further it was affected by the feeling that it is possible to establish a direct relation with God, Who is not to be regarded as a distant and All-Powerful Ruler of the destinies of mankind, but as a Friend and the Beloved of the soul. The mystics have desired to know God, so that they may love Him, and they have held that the soul can receive a revelation of God, by a direct religious experience—not through the senses or the intellect—and, by this means, enter into fellowship with Him.

They hold that if man can have this experience, there must be in him a share of the Divine Nature, that the soul is made to mirror the Splendour of God, and all things have a part in the Divine life. But the mystics all teach that no soul can have this direct experience of God, except by purification from self; the cleansing of the soul from self-love and from sensuality is essential for those who would attain to the Divine Wisdom and the Vision of God, for the perfection of Eternal Life, which they hold can be attained to here and now, is to see God in His Essence. Self can only be conquered by means of a greater love than self-love, and so the mystics have been the lovers of God, seeking the consummation of their love in Union with the Beloved.

Mysticism is not, however, theoretical but practical, teaching a Way of Life, to be followed by all who would win through to the goal, and this way is to be found following the same pattern, in East and West. There must first be the conversion of the mystic and discipline to get rid of the desires of the self, which will bring the external life into the form fitted for the seeker after God. After that comes the discipline of the inner life, bringing the thoughts and feeling and will into harmony with the eternal Will of God and making the mystic able to receive the Divine illumination. The soul is now able to attain to the life in God, that unitive state in which the soul shares, here and now, in eternal life.

There is an early tendency to asceticism and self-discipline to be found in Islām. The fast of Ramaḍān, the five daily prayers, the pilgrimage with its restrictions, the forbidding of wine, were all directed towards restraining the desires of the self and turning the mind towards the spiritual needs of the soul. This ascetic movement became associated with tendencies towards mysticism, which already had a place in Judaism and Christianity and the faiths of India. The Ṣūfīs—the name being taken from the garments of white wool (*ṣūf*) worn by the earliest ascetics—were those who devoted themselves to the life of self-renunciation, living in poverty and giving their time to prayer and meditation, who called themselves the " friends of God " (*awliyā allāh*), of whom a tradition says :—

" Verily, the friends of God fear nothing and grieve for nothing. For they look upon the inner reality of this world, while other men look upon its outward appearance. Also they look forward to the end of this world, while others look to the immediate present here. They destroy in it what they fear may destroy them, and abandon what they know will abandon them. They are hostile to those things with which other men make peace and bless the things which other men hate. They show the greatest admiration for the good deeds of others, while they themselves possess goods worthy of the greatest admiration. To them, knowledge is guidance, by which they themselves gain knowledge. They do not put faith except in that for which they hope, nor fear anything except that which should be avoided." This orthodox mysticism, among the Arabs, received its first definite consideration at the hands of Ḥārith b. Asad al-Muḥāsibī and it owes much to the ideal of asceticism found in Christianity, which taught the doctrine of complete renunciation and self-surrender to God, as leading to redemption.

The early Ṣūfīs were chiefly content with a way of Life, by which the carnal self (*nafs*) could be purified from its sins and weakness and the soul could enter on the path which led to God. On this path were certain stages, in which the soul could acquire qualities, which would lead it onwards and upwards to yet higher stages. These stages and stations, with their resultant qualities included repentance (*tawba*), patience (*ṣabr*), gratitude (*shukr*), hope (*rajā*) and fear (*khawf*), poverty (*faqr*), asceticism or renunciation (*zuhd*), the merging of the personal will with the Will of God (*tawḥīd*), dependence on, and trust in, God (*tawakkul*), love (*maḥabba*)—including longing for God (*shawq*), fellowship with Him (*uns*) and satisfaction with all He desires (*riḍā'*).

Of Love the Ṣufīs have much to say: it is the " wine of life ", it leads to the ecstasy found in the immediate experience of God. This is " pure love ", free from all interested motive. One of these lovers was asked whence he came and whither he was going and answered that he came from the Beloved and was going to Him. Asked what he sought, he said that he sought to meet with the Beloved; his food and drink were the remembrance of the Beloved and longing for Him. When they asked him wherewith he was clothed, he replied that it was with the veil of the Beloved and that his countenance was pale because of separation from Him. When at last, in impatience, his questioners asked him how long he was going to speak of " the Beloved, the Beloved ", he replied that he would so speak until he saw the Face of the Beloved.

These stages on the way led to the knowledge of God, gnosis (*ma'rifa*), His gift which enables the mystic to contemplate Him, to attain the achievement (*tamkīn*) of the goal sought and to pass into the unitive life with Him, which is the end of the Path, the passing away of mortality (*fanā'*) and the entrance into immortality (*baqā'*).

While the earliest Ṣūfīs led a life of renunciation of the world and self-discipline, giving themselves to devotion and meditation and prayer, they also spent time in offering spiritual guidance to those who sought it. It was a way of life, which they believed would lead them to God and bring them into fellowship and communion with Him. But soon Ṣufism developed a theosophic doctrine, based on mysticism, which included conceptions of a philosophic type, concerned with the Nature of the Godhead and the relation of the human soul to God. The Ṣūfīs began to concern themselves with the possibility of the means by which the human could ascend to the Divine, and how this was to be accomplished, and with the life in union with God and all that the attainment of that goal would mean.

Towards the end of the ninth century of the Christian era and the beginning of the tenth, pantheistic ideas begin to appear in Ṣūfism, of a spiritualistic type. These pantheistic mystics held that God, the One Reality, dwelling in solitude, desired to share His Reality with others, to manifest His Beauty to those whom He created, and this led to the doctrine of the Divine universality and of an absolute Unity, which maintained that the glory of God is to be found in all things, but in varying degrees. So the One Reality, God, was believed to dwell and manifest itself everywhere and not least in the human soul, while this world was held to be but the mirror in which True Being was reflected. This pantheistic aspect of Ṣūfism was developed first in Persia.

Music and song were used by the Ṣūfīs as a means of stirring up religious feeling and much of the purest and most typical teaching of Ṣūfism is to be found in mystical poetry. Much of this is symbolical and expressed sometimes in sensuous form, as the best means of interpreting mystical experience. Love, in its effects, is compared with wine; while God is the Supreme Beauty, the ultimate Object of all true love, earthly love may be used as a type of the Divine love.

Because, to the Ṣūfīs, love was the real essence of all religion, most of them, but especially the later Ṣūfīs, were universalists, admitting all faiths to contain something of the truth and all worshippers, who were lovers of God, to be striving towards the same goal.

As an early writer on the subject points out, Ṣūfism and the knowledge of God are founded on saintship and the saints (*awliyā*) are the chosen among the Ṣūfīs (*khuṣūṣ al-khuṣūṣ*), who have followed the Path to the end and attained to the unitive life. They are the " friends of God ", whom He has chosen, so that He may act through them : freed from the passions of the carnal self, their fellowship is with Him alone, and because their will is one with His, they can intercede with God, for their fellow-men, and their prayers are answered. Prayer was made to the saints even after their death, seeking their meditation on behalf of the living, and pilgrimages were made to their tombs, which were greatly venerated.

Ṣūfism, therefore, came to be a school for saints and the saint, in nearly every case, became a teacher and spiritual guide to a small or a large group of disciples. This led on to the formation of the great religious orders of Islām, which claimed as their founders the great Ṣūfī saints, some of whom, like the saints of other faiths, were not only possessed of great spiritual gifts, but also of practical ability in administration and power in human affairs.

The Ṣūfīs have included many types of character, from the simple unlettered saint, who had had no teacher, such as the woman Rābi'a al-'Adawiyya, whose teaching is quoted by many subsequent Ṣūfīs, to the distinguished scholar, with the best education of the day, who had travelled widely and come into contact with all those who could help him in the task of understanding Ṣūfism, who in the end found that it was a matter of personal experience, such as the great al-Ghazālī and others. All found alike that the soul must search after God and the search, after the way had been traversed with patience and humility and always with the surrender of the soul to the Divine guidance, would lead to the attainment of the end sought, the life in God.

ḤASAN AL-BAṢRĪ (110/728)

Ḥasan al-Baṣrī was born at Medina and brought up at Baṣra. He was well known for the austerity of his life and also for his sermons, preached at Baghdad. He was the one who laid the foundation of the "science of hearts" (*'ilm al-qulūb*), later developed by other Ṣūfīs.

1

Sell this present world of yours for the next world and you will gain both in entirety, but do not sell the next world for this world, for so shall you lose the two together. Act towards this world as if it were not, and towards the world to come as if it would never cease to be. He is a wise man who regards this world as nothing, and so regarding it, seeks the other world, instead of setting at nought the other world and seeking this. Whoso knows God regards Him as a friend and whoso knows this world regards Him as an enemy.

2

He who is content, needing nothing, and who has sought solitude, apart from mankind, will find peace: he who has trodden his carnal desires underfoot, will find freedom: he who has rid himself of envy will find friendship, and he who has patience for a little while will find himself prepared for Eternity.

God has said: "When My servant becomes altogether occupied with Me, then I make his happiness consist in the remembrance of Myself, and when I have made his happiness and his delight consist in that remembrance, he desires Me and I desire him, and when he desires Me and I desire him, I raise the veils between Me and him and I become manifest before his eyes. These do not forget Me, when others forget."

IBRĀHĪM B. ADHAM (160/777)

Ibrāhīm b. Adham was born at Balkh, the son of a king of Khurāsān. He was converted by hearing a Divine voice, while out hunting, and thenceforward lived a life of poverty and asceticism, living on the work of his hands. His teaching was concerned mainly with asceticism, but also with mysticism and he concerned himself especially with meditation (*murāqaba*) and gnosis (*ma'rifa*).

3

To become a saint of God you must covet nothing in this world or the next and you must give yourself entirely to God and turn your face to Him, having no desire for this world or for the world to come. To covet this world means to turn away from God, for the sake of what is transitory, and to covet the next world means turning away from God, for the sake of what is everlasting. What is transitory passes away and its renunciation also perishes, but the renunciation of what is everlasting does not pass away.

4

A certain man was constantly bewailing his condition and complaining of his poverty. Ibrāhīm b. Adham said to him: "My son, perhaps you paid but little for your poverty?" "You are talking nonsense," said the man, "you should be ashamed of yourself. Does anyone buy poverty?" Ibrāhīm replied: "For my part, I chose it of my own free will, nay, more I bought it at the price of this world's sovereignty, and I would buy one instant of this poverty again with a hundred worlds, for every moment it becomes worth yet more to me. When I found this precious merchandise, I bade a final farewell to royalty. Without any doubt, I know the value of poverty, while you remain in ignorance of it. I give thanks for it, while you are ungrateful. Those who aspire to spiritual things are willing to stake both body and soul in the search for them, and they spend their years consumed by their love to God. The bird of their ambition has attained to fellowship with Him: it has soared beyond temporal and spiritual things alike. If you are not man enough for such an ambition, get you gone, for you are unworthy to be a partaker of the Divine grace."

RĀBI'A AL-'ADAWIYYA (185/801)

Rābi'a was born at Baṣra. She is described by her biographer as "that woman who lost herself in union with the Divine, that one accepted by men as a second spotless Mary". As a child she was kidnapped and sold as a slave, but set free by her master, when he realised that she was one of God's elect. She then devoted herself to prayer and the service of God. Rābi'a had many disciples, who sought her counsel and her prayers. She was one of the earliest Ṣūfīs of whom we hear and her teaching is that of a real mystic.

5

One day Rābi'a was seen carrying fire in one hand and water in the other and she was running with speed. They asked her what was the meaning of her action and where she was going. She replied: "I am going to light a fire in Paradise and pour water on to Hell, so that both veils (i.e. hindrances to the true vision of God) may completely disappear from the pilgrims, and their purpose may be sure, and the servants of God may see Him, without any object of hope or motive of fear. What if the hope of Paradise and the fear of Hell did not exist? Not one could worship his Lord or obey Him."

6

The best thing for the servant, who desires to be near his Lord, is to possess nothing in this world or the next, save Him. I have not served God from fear of Hell, for I should be like a wretched hireling, if I did it from fear: nor from love of Paradise, for I should be a bad servant if I served for the sake of what was given, but I have served Him only for the love of Him and out of desire for Him.

The Neighbour first and then the house: is it not enough for me that I am given leave to worship Him? Even if Heaven and Hell were not, does it not behove us to obey Him? He is worthy of worship without any intermediate motive.

O my Lord, if I worship Thee from fear of Hell, burn me in Hell; and if I worship Thee from hope of Paradise, exclude me thence; but if I worship Thee for Thine own sake, then withhold not from me Thine Eternal Beauty.

7

The groaning and the yearning of the lover of God will not be satisfied until it is satisfied in the Beloved.

I have made Thee the Companion of my heart,
But my body is available for those who desire its
company.
And my body is friendly towards its guests,
But the Beloved of my heart is the Guest of my soul.

My peace is in solitude, but my Beloved is always with me. Nothing can take the place of His love and it is the test for me among mortal beings. Whenever I contemplate His Beauty, He is my *miḥrāb,*[1] towards Him is my *qibla*[2]—O Healer of souls, the heart feeds upon its desire and it is the striving towards union with Thee that has healed my soul. Thou art my Joy and my Life to eternity. Thou wast the source of my life, from Thee came my ecstasy. I have separated myself from all created beings: my hope is for union with Thee, for that is the goal of my quest.

ABŪ 'ABDALLAH A. B. 'ĀṢIM AL-ANṬĀKĪ
(220/835)

al-Anṭākī belonged to Antioch, in Syria. He was a well-known writer on asceticism and mysticism. Among his works was an early tract on the rules of interior discipline for our actions. He was called the "Explorer of Hearts" (*jāsūs al-qulūb*), because of his insight.

8

Avoid covetousness by preferring contentment: make sure of the sweetness of asceticism by cutting short hope: destroy the motives to desire by despairing altogether of the creatures; secure peace of mind by trust in God

[1] A niche in the mosque, facing towards Mecca.
[2] The part towards which the congregation direct their prayers.

(*tafwīḍ*): extinguish the fires of desire by the coldness of despair: close the road to pride by the knowledge of assured faith (*yaqīn*): seek peace of body by finding rest for the heart: secure peace of mind through ceasing to contend and abandoning the search for one's own good. Acquire kindliness by continuous association with those worshippers of God who are also wise, and enlightenment by continuous contrition, the door to which is opened by long reflection, while the habit of reflection is to be acquired in solitary retreat. The most harmful time for speech is when silence would be better for you and the most harmful time for silence is when speech would be more fitting for you and more necessary. That which brings you nearest to God is the abandonment of secret sins, because if you fail inwardly, both your outward and inward acts are made void.

9

Justice is of two kinds, the outward justice between yourself and the creature, and the inward justice between yourself and God. The road of justice is the road of rectitude, but the road of grace is the road of perfection. The most profitable part of reason is that which makes known to you the grace of God towards you and helps you to give thanks for it and rises up to oppose sensuality. The most profitable part of sincerity is the fact that it keeps you from hypocrisy and affectation and vainglory and that you do not like to be remembered for what you do and that you act without seeking reward for your action from any but God.

(10)

The signs of love to God include little exterior devotion

but continual reflection and the taste for solitude and silence. When others look at the lover, he does not see them: when he is called, he does not hear: when misfortune comes upon him, he is not grieved, and when success looks him in the face, he does not rejoice. He fears no one, puts hope in no man and makes no request of anyone (save God).

Act, then, as if there were no one on earth but yourself and no one in Heaven but God. All actions are to be guided by knowledge and true knowledge comes through the light of certainty, by which God enlightens the heart of His servant, so that he beholds the things of the spiritual world, and by the power of that light all the veils between him and that world are removed until, at last, by means of that radiance, he attains to contemplation of the Invisible.

HĀRITH B. ASAD AL-MUḤĀSIBĪ (243/857)

al-Muḥāsibī was born at Baṣra and educated at Baghdad where he gained a thorough knowledge of theology and philosophy, as well as Ṣūfism, and had some contact with Christian and Jewish teaching. He was called "al-Muḥāsibī" because of his practice of self-examination and he was said to be a Ṣūfī "whose arrow attained its mark". He was a great teacher and had many disciples who, in their turn, became great Ṣūfīs. He has left many writings on Ṣūfism.

11

What have you to do with delight in this world? It is the prison of the believer and he does not rejoice in it nor find pleasure in it. This world is only an abode of affliction, a place of care and sorrow, as Adam said: "We were begotten of God, as the offspring of God, and Satan has taken us captive through sin." It is not fitting for us to rejoice nor meet for us to do otherwise than weep and be grieved while we are in the abode of captivity and to continue so doing until we return to the abode from which we were taken captive. O my brothers, it is a shameful thing for an intelligent being to rejoice in any of the goods of this world and how should he rejoice in the praise of a man who is vain and deluded? Then understand what I say to you, O servant of God, you who are gratified by praise. Even though your good works were to win for you the friendship of all the birds of the heavens and the wild beasts and the cattle and the reptiles that creep on the earth, and though the angels were to praise you therefor, and men and jinns were all to rejoice in your company and praise you in what you did, and you were known thereby and your righteousness was commended, what reliance can you or any other place upon that? For it is only when you come to appear before God, that you will know the truth of the matter and whether God is pleased with you or not, and this alone is of consequence to you.

Your pleasure in the sweetness of sweet food you find only in eating it. The pleasure of lust and sensuality is in the thought and pursuit of it, and the pleasure of hypocrisy is in the infection of the heart by it; therefore it is necessary to make the will sound and in all action to contemplate God alone.

12

God has appointed self-mortification for the seeker, for the training of his soul. Men are ignorant of the high station of that one who is preoccupied with his Lord, who is seen to be thinking little of this world, who is humble, fearful, sorrowful, weeping, showing a meek spirit, keeping far from the children of this world, suffering oppression and not seeking revenge, despoiled, yet not desiring requital. He is dishevelled, dusty, shabby, thinking little of what he wears, wounded, alone, a stranger—but if the ignorant man were to look upon the heart of that seeker, and see how God has fulfilled in him what He promised of His favour and what He gives him in exchange for that which he renounced of the vain glory of this world and its pleasure, he would desire to be in that one's place, and would realise that it is he, the seeker after God, who is truly rich, and fair to look upon, who tastes delight, who is joyous and happy, for he has attained his desire and has secured that which he sought from his Lord. Let him who wishes to be near to God abandon all that alienates him from God.

13

What predominates in the heart of the mystic while he is at prayer is his sense of the mystery of Him in Whose Presence he stands and the might of Him Whom he seeks and the love of Him Who favours him with familiar intercourse with Himself, and he is conscious of that until he has finished praying, and he departs with a face so changed, that his friends would not recognise him, because of the awe that he feels at the Majesty of God. It is so that one who comes into the presence of some king, or someone for whom he yearns and whom he fears, stands in his presence, with a different attitude from what was his before he entered and goes out with an altered countenance. And how should it not be so with the Lord of the Worlds, Who has not ceased to be, nor will cease to be, He Who hath no equal ?

For every human heart there are paths—diverse interests leading out in all directions, and he who follows these paths cannot give his mind to God. Whichever way he follows, he will perish and fall. Blessed is that servant whose heart is not pre-occupied with anything save his Lord Most High, whose thoughts are concentrated on Him alone.

14

Meditation is the gate of gnosis—though the servant were to serve God with outward acts of devotion for a thousand years and a thousand years again and then were not acquainted with the practice of meditation, all his service would but increase his distance from God and increase the hardness of his heart and diminish his faith. Meditation is the chief possession of the gnostic, that whereby the sincere and the God-fearing make progress on the journey to God ; it brings comfort to the sorrowing and rest to those who have renounced all for His sake. It is a strength to the godly and a means of exaltation to the devout.

The chief part of the recollection of God is keeping close to Him. He who is preoccupied with God is separated from the creatures, and those who are detached from the creatures have escaped to the regions of solitude and are alone with the sweetness of the recollection of God, and in proportion as the heart enters into communion with God, through recollection, it escapes from loneliness. The servant contemplates his Lord, having cut off his hope from all save Him and he sees no place for his own choice, for God is sufficient for him and in Him he has found the peace of certainty. No station is higher than that in which the soul dwells with God in perfect tranquillity, because God is enough for it, and it looks unto Him and away from the creatures, having lost nothing and gained all things.

The contemplative no longer sees this world and what it contains, and no longer regards himself, for the sole object of his contemplation is God. It is all one to him whether he sails upon the sea or walks upon dry land whether he enjoys companionship or is alone, in his times of action or his times of rest, for God Most High is sufficient for him and life in Him preoccupies him from all else.

15

Fellowship with the Creator makes the saints also compassionate to His creatures, whom they would fain bring into their own happy state, for they themselves have chosen that better part which shall not be taken away. They feel no envy of earthly kings, for unto them is appointed eternal glory in the Presence of the King of kings, and though in the eyes of men they are despised, they are precious in His sight, and because now they count all things but loss for His sake, in the world to come, they shall be exalted with Him in glory. How should he be a stranger, who is in fellowship with his Lord, or why should separation and detachment from the conversation of men be grievous to the heart of him whose understanding and whose tongue are preoccupied with intercourse with God? There is nothing to be despised in him who has refused to lay up treasures on earth in order that he may secure unto himself the treasure of entrance into the Presence of his Lord, in the life everlasting.

16

When love is established in the heart of a servant, there is no place there for remembrance of men or demons or of Paradise or Hell, nor for anything except the remembrance of the Beloved and His grace. The love of God in its essence is really the illumination of the heart by joy because of its nearness to the Beloved, for love, in solitude, rises up triumphant and the heart of the lover is possessed by the sense of its fellowship with Him, and when solitude is combined with secret intercourse with the Beloved, the joy of that intercourse overwhelms the mind, so that it is no longer concerned with this world and what is therein.

To that one whom God has placed in the rank of His lovers, He gives the Vision of Himself, for He has sworn, saying, " By My glory, I will show him My Face and I will heal his soul by the Vision of Myself ". The hearts of such lovers are held captive in the hidden shrine of the Divine loving-kindness : they are marked out by their knowledge of the revelation of the Divine Majesty, being transformed by the joy of the Vision, in contemplation of the Invisible, and of the enveloping Glory of God, and from them all hindrances are removed, for they tread the path of friendship with God and are transported into the garden of Vision, and their hearts dwell in that region, where they see without eyes, and are in the company of the Beloved, without looking upon Him, and converse with an Unseen Friend.

This is the description of the lovers of God, who do righteousness, who are gifted with heavenly wisdom, who are on their guard both night and day, pure in all their thoughts, those whom God has prepared for His service, whom He has preserved by His care, whom He has invested with His own authority. They are continually serving Him to Whom belong the heavens and the earth: they are completely satisfied, for they live the good life, their bliss is eternal and their joy is made perfect and they possess an everlasting treasure within their hearts, for it is as if they contemplated with the eye of the heart the Glory that is invisible, and God is the object and goal of their aspirations. Whoso knows God loves Him and whoso loves Him, He makes to dwell with Him and whom He makes to dwell with Him, in whom He dwells, blessed is he, yea blessed.

ABŪ SA'ĪD AḤMAD B. BASHR B. ZIYĀD B. AL-'ARĀBĪ (9th Century)

Aḥmad b. al-'Arābī was associated with the great Ṣūfīs of his time. He wrote a book on ecstasy (*Kitāb al-wajd*).

17

The beginning of ecstasy is the lifting of the veil and the vision of the Divine Guardian (*raqīb*), and the presence of understanding, and the contemplation of the invisible, and the discoursing on secret things and perceiving the non-existent, and it means, that you pass away from where you are. Ecstasy is the first of the stations of the elect and it is the inheritance of assurance of the thing desired, and for those who have experienced it, when its light has been shed abroad in their hearts, all doubt and suspicion have passed from them. He who is veiled from ecstasy and dominated by the claims of the self, is hampered by making a living and by worldly motives, for the self is veiled by such motives. But if these are banished and devotion to God is made pure from self-interest and the heart comes to itself again and is made refined and pure and gains benefit from exhortation, when it worships God and utters prayers in intimate converse with Him, drawing near to Him, and He addresses it and it hears with attention Him Who speaks, and is contemplating Him and its conscience is pure, then it beholds from what it was freed and there is ecstasy (*wajd*), because it has found what was lost.

Ecstasy in this world comes not from revelation, but consists in the vision of the heart and realisation of the truth and gaining assurance, and he who has attained to it beholds with the joy of certainty and with a devotion free of self-interest, for he is all-attentive. When he awakes from the vision, he loses what he has found, but his knowledge remains with him, and for a long time his spirit enjoys that, with the increase of certainty which he has gained through the vision. This depends upon the servant's proximity to his Lord, or his distance from Him, and upon the vision given to him by his Creator.

But if anyone asks for a further description of ecstasy, let him cease to do that, for how can a thing be described which has no description but itself, and no witness to it but itself, and its reality is known from itself, to him who has it: he knows of its existence from his ecstasy. He who does not know it, denies its existence and both he who knows it and he who does not know it, are altogether unable to deal with the matter. For it is felt by experience only, and he who has it can contemplate the vision and he is one of the chosen, truly existent, but inaccessible and lost, for he is veiled by his own light from its light, and by his own attributes from its apprehension and by the names by which he calls it, from its essence, I mean the essence of ecstasy, for certainty and faith and truth and likewise love and longing, and proximity—all that is but a poor description of it. He who asks about its flavour and experience asks about the impossible, for flavour and experience are not known by description, without tasting and experience.

ABU'L-FAYḌ THAWBĀN B. IBRĀHĪM DHU'L-NŪN AL-MIṢRĪ (245/859)

Dhu'l-Nūn was an Egyptian, who travelled widely in the study of Ṣūfism and was condemned for his public teaching of it. He was considered to be one of the "Hidden saints" and the spiritual head (*quṭb*) of the Ṣūfīs of his time. He was "possessed of great insight into the Divine mysteries and the doctrine of the Unity".

18

On my first journey I found a kind of knowledge acceptable to both the elect and the common folk, and on the second knowledge acceptable to the elect but not to the common folk, and on the third knowledge acceptable to neither the elect nor the common folk, and I remained an outcast and alone. The first kind of knowledge was repentance, which both the elect and the common folk accept, and the second was trust in God and fellowship with Him and love, which the elect accept, and the third was the knowledge of reality, which is beyond the power of human learning and reason to attain, so men reject it.

Knowledge is of three kinds: first, the knowledge of the Unity of God and this is common to all believers: second, knowledge gained by proof and demonstration, and this belongs to the wise and the eloquent and the learned, and third, knowledge of the attributes of the Unity, and this belongs to the saints, those who contemplate the Face of God within their hearts, so that God reveals Himself to them in a way in which He is not revealed to any others in the world.

19

I have seen nothing more conducive to righteousness than solitude, for he who is alone sees nothing but God, and if he sees nothing but God, nothing moves him but the will of God.

Every intercessor is veiled by his intercessions from contemplation of the Truth, for the Truth is present to the people of faith, since God Himself is the Creative Truth and His word is Truth and there is no need for anyone to make intercession, when God Himself is present with him and manifested to him. If He were absent, then should intercession be made to Him.

20

The gnostic becomes more humble every hour, for every hour he is drawing nearer to God. The gnostics see without knowledge, without sight, without information received, and without observation, without description, without veiling and without veil. They are not themselves, but in so far as they exist at all, they exist in God. Their movements are caused by God and their words are the words of God, which are uttered by their tongues, and their sight is the sight of God, which has entered into their eyes. So God Most High has said, " When I love a servant, I, the Lord, am his ear, so that He hears by Me ; I am his eye, so that he sees by Me, and I am his tongue, so that he speaks by Me, and I am his hand, so that he takes by Me ".

21

The saints are those whom God has invested with the radiance of His love and adorned with the fair mantle of His grace, upon whose heads He set the crown of His joy, and He put love towards them into the hearts of His creatures. Then He brought them forth, having entrusted to their hearts the treasures of the Invisible, which depend upon union with the Beloved, and their hearts are turned towards Him and their eyes behold the greatness of His Majesty. Then He made them seek for a remedy and He gave them knowledge of the places where the means of healing was to be found. He caused their disciples to be abstinent and God-fearing, and to them, His saints, He gave assurance of an answer to their prayers and He said : " O My saints, if there come to you one sick through separation from Me, heal him, or a fugitive from Me, seek him out, or afraid of Me, then reassure him, or desirous of union with Me, then show him favour, or seeking to approach Me, encourage him. If he is despairing of My grace, help him, or hoping for My loving kindness, give him good news, or with right thoughts of Me, then welcome him, or showing love to Me, show friendship unto him, or seeking to know My attributes, give him guidance. Or if he be doing evil in despite of My loving kindness, then remonstrate with him, or forgetful of it, then remind him. If anyone who is injured, ask help of you, give it to him and to him who joins you in My name, show friendship : if he goes astray, search for him, but if he would constrain you to sin, put him away from you.

O My saints, I have reasoned with you, and to you I have addressed Myself, towards you has been My desire and from you have I sought the fulfilment of My Will, for upon you has My choice been laid, and you have I predestined for My work. You have I appointed to serve Me and you have I chosen and made to be Mine elect.—To you have I given the most precious of rewards, the fairest of gifts, the greatest of graces. I am the Searcher of hearts, He Who knows the mysteries of the Invisible—I am the Object of your desire, I, Who read the secrets of the heart—Ye are My saints, My Beloved: ye are Mine and I am yours."

YAḤYA B. MU'ĀDH AL-RĀZĪ (258/871)

Yaḥya b. Mu'ādh al-Rāzī lived and died at Nīshāpūr. He was one of the first to give a public course of lectures on mysticism and also one of the first to declare directly his love for God, in verse. He was described as "this sea of verities, this guide of the '*ulemā*, this victorious athlete, this explorer of the road to God".

22

My God, of Thy mercy forgive me my sins. O my Lord, though my sinful deeds make me fear Thy justice, yet the greatness of Thy compassion makes me hope in Thee. O Lord, I have not merited Paradise by my deeds and I cannot endure the pains of Hell, so I entrust myself simply to Thy grace. If on the Day of Resurrection, I am asked: "What hast thou brought unto Me?" I shall reply: "What can one straight from prison, with unkempt hair and tattered garment, burdened with worldly cares and full of shame, bring unto Thee? Wash me from my sins, give unto me the robe of the redeemed, and in Thy mercy cast me not away from Thy Presence."

ABŪ YAZĪD ṬAYFŪR AL-BISṬĀMĪ, CALLED BĀYAZĪD BISṬĀMĪ (261/875)

Abū Yazīd al-Bisṭāmī was a Persian, belonging to Bisṭām, where he spent most of his life. He was an ascetic, given to solitude, whose one desire was to attain to a direct experience of the Divine Reality. He is much quoted by later writers and had a far-reaching influence upon the development of Ṣūfism, in the direction of a pantheistic doctrine.

23

It is related that one night Shaykh Bāyazīd went outside the city and found everything wrapped in deep silence, free from the clamour of men. The moon was shedding her radiance upon the world and by her light made night as brilliant as the day. Stars innumerable shone like jewels in the heavens above, each pursuing its appointed task. For a long time the Shaykh made his way across the open country and found no movement therein, nor saw a single soul. Deeply moved by this he cried: "O Lord, my heart is stirred within me by this Thy Court displayed in all its splendour and sublimity, yet none are found here to give Thee the adoring worship which is Thy due. Why should this be, O Lord?" Then the hidden voice of God spoke to him: "O thou who art bewildered in the Way, know that the King does not grant admission to every passer-by. So exalted is the Majesty of His Court that not every beggar can be admitted thereto. When the Splendour of My Glory sheds abroad its radiance from this My sanctuary, the heedless and those who are wrapped in the sleep of indolence are repelled thereby. Those who are worthy of admittance to this Court wait for long years, until one in a thousand of them wins entrance thereto."

24

At the beginning I was mistaken in four respects. I concerned myself to remember God, to know Him, to love Him and to seek Him. When I had come to the end I saw that He had remembered me before I remembered Him, that His knowledge of me had preceded my knowledge of Him, His love towards me had existed before my love to Him and He had sought me before I sought Him.

I thought that I had arrived at the very Throne of God and I said to it: "O Throne, they tell us that God rests upon thee." "O Bāyazīd," replied the Throne, "we are told here that He dwells in a humble heart."

For thirty years God Most High was my mirror, now I am my own mirror and that which I was I am no more, for "I" and "God" represents polytheism, a denial of His Unity. Since I am no more, God Most High is His own mirror. Behold, now I say that God is the mirror of myself, for with my tongue He speaks and I have passed away.

25

While I was asleep, it seemed to me that I ascended to the heavens in quest of God, seeking union with God Most Glorious, so that I might abide with Him for ever, and I was tested by a trial. God displayed before me gifts of all kinds and offered me dominion over the whole heaven, and yet I turned aside my eyes from this, because I knew that He was testing me thereby, and I turned not towards it, out of reverence for the holiness of my Lord and I said in regard to it all: " O my Beloved, my desire is other than that which is offered to me." Then I ascended to the Second Heaven and saw winged angels, who fly a hundred thousand times each day to the earth, to look upon the saints of God, and their faces shone like the sun. I travelled on and when I had reached the Seventh Heaven, one called unto me: " O Abū Yazīd, stop, stop, for you have reached the goal," but I paid no heed to his words and I pursued my quest. And when God Most High realised the sincerity of my desire to seek Him, He turned me into a bird, and I went on flying, past kingdom after kingdom, and desert after desert, and plain after plain and sea after sea, and veil after veil, until behold the angel of the footstool of God met me with a pillar of light and said to me, " Take it " and I took it. And lo, the heavens and all that were therein sought refuge in the shadow of my gnosis, and sought light in the light of my longing, yet all the angels seemed but as a gnat, compared with my all-absorbing concern with the search for God.

So I continued to fly, until I reached the footstool of God, and lo, I was met by angels, whose eyes were as the number of the stars of heaven, and from each eye shone forth light and those lights became lamps and I heard sounding forth from each lamp, " Glory to God " and " There is no God but God ". Then I went on flying until I arrived at a sea of light, with waves beating against one another, and beside it the light of the sun would seem dark, and upon the sea were ships of light, compared with which the light of those waters appeared to be darkness. I continued to cross sea upon sea until I reached the greatest of seas, upon which stands the Throne of the All-Merciful. I went on swimming therein, until I beheld, looking from the Empyrean to the earth beneath, the cherubim and those who bore up the Throne, and all whom God has created both in heaven and earth, as less than a mustard-seed floating between the heavens and the earth, in comparison with the flight of my spirit in the quest for God.

And when God Most-Glorious perceived the sincerity of my desire to seek Him, He called to me and said: "O My chosen one, approach unto Me and ascend to the heights of My glory and the plains of My splendour and sit upon the carpet of My holiness, so that thou mayst see the working of My grace in my appointed time. Thou art My chosen and My beloved and My elect among the creatures." Then I began to melt away, as lead melts in the heat of the fire. Then He gave me to drink from the fountain of Grace in the cup of fellowship and changed me into a state beyond description and brought me near unto Him, and so near did He bring me that I became nearer unto Him than the spirit to the body. I continued thus until I became even as the souls of men had been, in that state before existence was and God abode in solitude apart, without created existence or space or direction or mode of being—may His glory be exalted and His Name sanctified.

ABŪ SAʻĪD AḤMAD B. ʻĪSĀ AL-KHARRĀZ
(286/899)

Abū Saʻīd al-Kharrāz was a Baghdadī by origin and was said to be the first who spoke about the doctrine of annihilation (*fanā'*) and abiding (*baqā'*). He wrote a book on " What is fitting in Prayer " (*Adab al-Ṣalāt*) and the " Book of Sincerity " (*Kitāb al-Ṣidq*), one of the earliest treatises on Ṣūfism, written by a Ṣūfī.

26

When entering on Prayer you should come into the Presence of God as you would on the Day of Resurrection, when you will stand before Him with no mediator between, for He welcomes you and you are in confidential talk with Him and you know in whose Presence you are standing, for He is the King of kings. When you have lifted your hands and said : " God is most Great ", then let nothing remain in your heart save glorification, and let nothing be in your mind in the time of glorification, than the glory of God Most High, so that you forget this world and the next, while glorifying Him.

When a man bows in prayer, then it is fitting that he should afterwards raise himself, then bow again and make intercession, until every joint of his body is directed towards the Throne of God and this means that he glorifies God Most High until there is nothing in his heart greater than God Most Glorious and he thinks so little of himself that he feels himself to be less than a mote of the dust. When he raises his head and praises God, he knows that He is listening to him, and when he worships it is fitting for him so to worship that there is nothing in his heart nearer to him than God. For when the servant is near to his Lord in worship, he should keep his tongue from what is inconsistent with that and there should be in his heart none greater than He nor more glorious. His prayer is thus made perfect and he will be full of awe and reverence, so that he ceases to be conscious of other things and while in prayer he will not be concerned with anything else and he does not occupy himself with any thing except Him in Whose Presence he stands while at prayer.

27

The gnostics are the treasure-houses of God: He deposits in them the knowledge of mysteries and information concerning wonderful things, and they speak of them with the tongue of eternity and interpret them with an interpretation which is everlasting. If God desires to be united with a servant of His, He opens to him the gate of worship, and if he delights in worship, He opens to him the gate of proximity, then He raises him to the station of fellowship, then He seats him on the throne of unification (*tawḥīd*). Then He raises the veil from him and makes him enter into His own Unicity and unveils to him His Glory and Majesty, and when the servant's eyes fall upon the glory and Majesty of God, he remains outside of himself and he comes into the care of God and is freed from self for ever.

The first stage for that one who has found the knowledge of unification and the assurance of that, is that there passes from his heart the remembrance of all things and he becomes alone with God Most High. For the first stage of unification is that the servant gives up everything and returns all things to Him to Whom they belong and that He is in control of them and makes them subject to Himself. So then the remembrance of all things passes from the servant's heart and the remembrance of God Most High takes possession of it—the heart—and the remembrance of things passes from his heart in the remembrance of God Most Glorious.

From one who contemplates God in his heart is hidden all else and all things are reduced to nought and he passes away into the Presence of God's Majesty and there remains nothing in his heart save God alone.

Blessed is the man who has drunk of the cup of His love and tasted the joy of communion with God Most Glorious and has approached Him with delight in his love for Him. His heart is filled with love and, full of joy, he has approached God and come to Him, full of longing for Him. How great is his yearning love and longing for his Lord! He has no abode save in Him nor any intimate friend save Him.

AḤMAD B. M. ABU'L-ḤUSAYN AL-NŪRĪ
(295/907)

al-Nūrī was a great ascetic and teacher of Baghdad. He was said to bear the name of "Nūrī", because by the light (*nūr*) of intuition he was able to interpret mysteries and even to read the thoughts of his disciples. He was persecuted for his adherence to Ṣūfism.

28

Ṣūfism is enmity to this world and friendship with the Lord: he who worships God is in contemplation of Him.

The mind is weak and it can deal only with what is weak like itself. When God created the reason He said to it: "Who am I?" and it was silent. Then He shed upon it the light of His Unicity (*waḥdāniyya*) and it said: "Thou art God"; and it is not for the reason to know God except by God. He who does not know God in this world will not know Him in the next.

The mystic ecstasy is a flame kindled in the heart by

longing for the Beloved and whether it arises from joy or grief it brings remembrance of Him. Love is the rending of the veil and the revelation of what is hidden from the eyes of men. I looked one day at the Light and I did not cease looking at it until I became the Light.

'AMR B. 'UTHMĀN AL-MAKKĪ (297/909)

al-Makkī was a well-known Ṣūfī and the writer of a "Book of Contemplation" (*Kitāb al-Mushāhada*) and a "Book of Love" (*Kitāb al-Maḥabba*).

29

God created the hearts seven thousand years before the bodies and kept them in the station of proximity (*qurb*) to Himself and He created the spirits seven thousand years before the hearts and kept them in the garden of intimate fellowship (*uns*) with Himself, and the consciences —the innermost part—He created seven thousand years before the spirits and kept them in the degree of union (*waṣl*) with Himself. Then He imprisoned the conscience in the spirit and the spirit in the heart and the heart in the body. Then He tested them—and sent prophets —and then each began to seek its own station. The body occupied itself with prayer, the heart attained to love, the spirit arrived at proximity to its Lord and the inmost part found rest in union with Him.

The hearts of the gnostics contemplate God unceasingly and with assurance and they see Him in everything and all things that exist in Him. He is ever present to their contemplation and they are absent (in spirit) while present (in the body), and present while absent, for they dwell apart with God, whether they are absent or present, and they contemplate Him openly and in secret and at the last as at the first.

ABU'L-QĀSIM B. M. AL-JUNAYD (298/910)

al-Junayd was a Persian by origin, but was born and brought up in Baghdad. He became one of the most famous of all the Ṣūfī teachers, though he would talk with only a small number, as few as ten. The Ṣūfī doctrines were developed and systematised by him and he wrote a number of mystical works, among them the " Book of Annihilation " (*Kitāb al-Fanā'*), the " Book on Unification " (*Kitāb al-Tawḥīd*) and the " Book on the Remedy for Souls " (*Kitāb Dawā' al-arwāḥ*).

30

The journey from this world to the next (i.e. to give up worldly things for spiritual things) is easy for the believer : the journey from the creatures (i.e. separation from them and from dependence on them) to the Creator is hard : the journey from the self to God is very hard : and to be able to abide in God is harder still.

Ṣūfism means that God makes you to die to yourself and makes you alive in Him. It is to purify the heart from the recurrence of creaturely temptations, to say farewell to all the natural inclinations, to subdue the qualities which belong to human nature, to keep far from the claims of the senses, to adhere to spiritual qualities, to ascend by means of Divine knowledge, to be occupied with that which is eternally the best, to give wise counsel to all people, faithfully to observe the truth, and to follow the Prophet in respect of the religious law.

31

Love means that the attributes of the lover are changed into those of the Beloved. Now he lives in accordance with the saying of God: "When I love him, I will be his eye by which he sees and his hearing by which he hears and his hand by which he reaches out."

The saint who desires to attain to the unification of the human will with the Divine Will (which is the preliminary to complete union), should be as a dead body in the hands of God, acquiescing in all the vicissitudes which come to pass through His decree and all that is brought about by the might of His power, for the saint is submerged in the ocean of Unity, by passing away from himself and from the demands of the creatures upon himself and from all response to them, into the realisation of the Unicity of God, into the direct experience of His Presence. He leaves behind him his own feelings and actions, as he passes into the life with God, and so becomes that which God desired for him, that the servant, at the last, should return to the state in which he was at first, and should become as he was before he began to be.

32

God gives to the gnostic the ardent desire to behold His Essence, then knowledge becomes vision and vision revelation, and revelation contemplation and contemplation existence—with and in God. Words are hushed to silence, life becomes death, explanations (which are necessary for finite minds in this world), come to an end, signs (which are a concession to those who are weak in faith), are effaced. Mortality (*fanā'*) is ended and immortality (*baqā'*) is made perfect. Weariness and care cease, the elements perish and there remains what will not cease, as time that is timeless ceases not.

The spirits of the gnostics rejoice in communion with the Unseen, abiding in the Presence of the All-Glorious, the Pre-eminent, in the cloud of glory which envelops Him, in the shadow of His holiness. They have attained to a high station and they pass on thence to yet greater perfection, to an absolute glory which is immaterial, and they walk, clad in the mantle of Unification.

ḤUSAYN B. MANṢŪR AL-ḤALLĀJ (309/922)

al-Ḥallāj was a Persian by birth. Because he could read the secret thoughts of men he was called "the Carder of consciences" (*Ḥallāj al-asrār*). He went to Baghdad and there, after a long imprisonment for preaching heretical doctrines, he was put to a cruel death.

33

O Lord, from Whom all good is hoped for, and Who art sought out in all afflictions and from Whom men seek the fulfilment of every need: from Thee they seek the generous forgiveness of every guilty deed and Thy pity. Thou knowest all things which we know not and Thou seest all things, which we cannot do, as Thou discernest what is secret and dost look into the consciences of Thy creation: Thou hast power over all things.

Because of what I have found of the flowing forth of Thy love and the fragrance of Thy proximity, I feel contempt for the firm mountains and the earth and the heavens. If Thou wert to offer to sell me Paradise for a moment of my time with Thee, or for one moment of the least of my spiritual states, I would not buy it.

If Thou wert to place before me Hell-fire, with all it contains of torment, I would think lightly of it in comparison with my state when Thou art hidden from me. Forgive the people and do not forgive me, and have mercy upon them and do not have mercy upon me. I do not intercede with Thee for myself nor beseech Thee for what is due to me. Do with me what Thou wilt.

34

The Ṣūfī is he who aims, from the first, at reaching God, the Creative Truth. Until he has found what he sought, he takes no rest, nor does he give heed to any person. For Thy sake I haste over land and water: over the plain I pass and the mountain I cleave and from everything I meet I turn my face, until the time when I reach that place where I am alone with Thee.

I am He Whom I love and He Whom I love is I,
We are two spirits indwelling one body.
When thou seest me, thou seest Him,
And when thou seest Him, then thou dost see us both.

‘ABD AL-JABBĀR IBN AL-ḤUSAYN AL-NIFFARĪ (354/965)

al-Niffarī was probably of ‘Irāqi origin and seems to have spent part of his life as a wandering dervish. He was known as a Ṣūfī and recognised as a great teacher of the mystic Way. He died in Egypt. His best-known works are the "Book of the Stations" (*Kitāb al-Mawāqif*) and the "Book of Addresses" (*Kitāb al-Mukhāṭabāt*).

35

The Lord said unto me: "Ask me and say, ‘O Lord,

how long shall I hold fast to Thee, so that when my day of judgment comes, Thou wilt not chastise me with Thy chastisement, and Thou wilt not turn Thy Face from me'? and I shall say to thee, 'Hold fast to the religious law (*Sunna*) in knowledge and action, and hold fast also to the knowledge which I have given thee in the innermost parts of thy heart, and know that when I have made Myself known to thee, I will not accept from thee anything of the religious law except what came to thee from My making Myself known to thee, because thou art one to whom I have spoken. Thou hast listened to Me, thou dost know that thou hearest Me and thou dost see that all things are from Me.'"

36

When I have concentrated thy characteristics and thy heart on nothing but the Vision of Myself, what hast thou to do with supplications? Wilt thou ask Me to take the veil away? I have taken it away. Or wilt thou ask Me to veil Myself? With whom then wilt thou go on thy way?

And He said unto me: "When thou hast seen Me, there remain for thee only two requests. Thou canst ask of Me in My absence to keep thee in the contemplation of Me, and thou canst ask Me, when thou hast that Vision of Me, that thou mayst say to a thing, 'Be' and it shall be."

37

Does not unveiling consist in this, that thou shouldst free thyself from all other things and the knowledge of them and that thou shouldst behold Me through that whereby I have revealed Myself to thee, and nothing that is hostile to us should trouble thee and no familiar friend should keep thee for his own purpose, whilst I give thee the Vision of Myself and make Myself known unto thee, though it be but once in thy lifetime, making known to thee My friendship for thee ? For thou hast renounced all things because of what I have revealed to thee, so that thou art Mine and nothing separates thee from Me, and thou cleavest to Me alone (for what cleaves to you does not to Me), and this is the description of those who are My friends, the saints, so know that thou art one of them.

38

Eternity sings praises to Me and it is one of My attributes that it should do so, and I have created from its praise the night and day and I have made them both into veils stretched over men's eyes and thoughts, and over their minds and hearts. Night and day are two veils spread out over all that I have created, but because I have chosen thee for Myself, I have lifted the two veils that thou mightest see Me and thou hast seen Me, therefore stand in thy place before Me and continue in the Vision of Me, for otherwise thou wilt be snatched away by everything that happens to distract thee. So stand firm and attribute to Me alone all which I have manifested to thee.

IKHWĀN AL-ṢAFĀ (10th century)

The Ikhwān al-Safā, the Brethren of Purity, were a group of philosophers, whose philosophy was directed towards the attainment of knowledge of the Godhead. They taught the doctrine of emanation and believed that all good things were the gift of the Divine grace and that human souls were illuminated by the Divine Light. These men compiled a great Encyclopædia of some fifty treatises, teaching at the end a mystical doctrine of the nature of the Godhead.

39

Then know that all those benefits and excellencies and good things come only from the Divine grace and the shedding of His light upon Universal Mind, and from Universal Mind it is shed upon Universal Soul and from Universal Soul upon material things. These material things are forms which are seen by human beings in the material world, who see individuals and the heavenly bodies coming forth from the heavenly sphere to the boundary of the earth. Then know that the penetration of those good gifts and benefits from their beginning to their end, is like the penetration of the light and splendour which is seen in the night, when there is a new moon coming forth from the essential substance of the moon, upon the empty space. Now that light which is upon the substance of the moon, comes from the sun, and that which is upon the substance of the sun and all the stars comes from the irradiation of Universal Soul, and that which falls upon Universal Soul comes from Universal Mind, and that which falls upon Universal Mind, from the Divine grace and from the Splendour of God. It is evident from what we have said that God is the universal Object of love, and that all existent things long for Him and seek to approach Him, and that all things return to Him, because through Him they exist and through Him they subsist and endure and continue to be, and are perfected, for He is the Absolute One Existent and to Him belong immortality and eternity and consummate and complete perfection.

40

But the friends of God, who are the saints, and who are His holy ones, and the wise, who are gnostics, possessed of insight, see Him and contemplate Him in all their mystic states and conditions by night and day. He is not hidden from them, for a single moment, just as what He has made and His creatures and what He has made manifest, are not hidden from the eyes of those who see . . Not the particle of an atom in the heavens nor on the earth is remote from Him, nor anything smaller even than that, or larger, but He is present with them, wherever they are. God opens the hearts of His saints and makes them assured of the truth of their gnosis and He gives light to their eyes and takes the veil away from them, so that they see Him and contemplate Him with their eyes, just as they have known Him in their hearts.

ABŪ NAṢR AL-SARRĀJ (378/988)

Abū Naṣr al-Sarrāj was born at Ṭūs and was one of the earliest systematic writers on Ṣūfism. He travelled widely in the desire to meet and converse with Ṣūfīs and was himself a spiritual director. His only known work is the "Book Giving Light on Ṣūfism" (*Kitāb al-Luma' fi'l-taṣawwuf*). Quoting the opinion of the Ṣūfīs, he also gives his own view on the subject.

41

Renunciation (*zuhd*) is a noble station and it is the basis of all spiritual progress. It is the first step on the way for those who set their faces towards God, those who seek to consecrate themselves to His service alone, to carry out His Will and to trust completely to Him. That one who does not base his practice of religion on renunciation cannot hope to make any progress therein, for the love of this world leads to all sin, and the renunciation of it leads to all good deeds and to obedience to the Will of God.

42

Before the time of Prayer comes, the servant must be in a state of preparation and his attitude must be that which is essential for prayer, namely a state of meditation and recollection, free from wandering thoughts and consideration or remembrance of anything save God alone. Those who enter in this way upon prayer, with heart intent only upon God, will proceed from prayer to prayer, in that same state of recollection and will remain in that state after they have ceased to pray.

43

Gnosis is fire and faith light, gnosis is ecstasy and faith a gift. The difference between the believer and the gnostic is that the believer sees by the light of God and the gnostic sees by means of God Himself, and the believer has a heart, but the gnostic has no heart: the heart of the believer finds rest in worship, but the gnostic finds no rest save in God. Gnosis is of three kinds, the gnosis of acceptance, the gnosis of reality, and the gnosis of contemplation, and in the gnosis of contemplation, understanding and learning and explanation and disputation pass away.

"Passing away" and "continuance" are two terms which are both applicable to the servant who acknowledges that God is One and who makes the ascent into unification from the stage of the common folk to the stage of the elect. The meaning of "passing away" and "continuance" in its beginning, is the passing away of ignorance into the abiding condition of knowledge and the passing away of disobedience into the abiding state of obedience, and the passing away of indifference into the state of continual worship, and the passing away of the consideration of the actions of the servant, which are temporary, into the vision of the Divine Grace, which is eternal.

ABŪ BAKR AL-KALĀBĀDHĪ (385/995)

Little is known about al-Kalābādhī, except of his work, but Bukhārā seems to have been his native place and he was buried there. He wrote the "Book of Inquiry as to The Religion of the Ṣūfīs" (*Kitāb al-Ta'arruf li Madhhab ahl al-Taṣawwuf*), which was accepted as an authoritative textbook on Ṣūfī doctrine.

44

The real meaning of detachment (*tajrīd*) is to be separated outwardly from all possessions and inwardly from what is unreal. It is to take nothing from what belongs to this world, nor to seek anything in exchange for the transitory things which have been renounced, not even eternity itself. That renunciation has been made for the sake of the One True God, for no cause or reason save Him alone—It means also that one's heart should be detached from consideration of different stages and states, in which one remains at different times, and should feel no satisfaction in them or desire for them. The one who breaks the fetters of self-hood, through passing away from self, is the one chosen to approach God and he becomes alone with the One Reality.

45

Love is of two natures, the love which is tranquil, which is found among both the elect and the common folk, and the love which is rapture, which is found only among the elect. This is the road which leads direct to God: therein is found no vision of the self or the creaturely, nor any vision of motives or of states, but the lover is absorbed in the Vision of God and what is from Him.

The meaning of union (*ittiṣāl*) is that the heart should be separated from all save God and should glorify none save Him and hearken to none save Him—It means the heart's attachment to the state in which it is occupied by the glory of the One to the exclusion of all else.

ABŪ ṬĀLIB AL-MAKKĪ (386/996)

Abū Ṭālib al-Makkī lived and taught in Mecca, Baṣra and Baghdad. He was the author of an early treatise on Ṣūfism, "The Food of Hearts" (*Qūt al-Qulūb*). He is a careful writer and one held to be of great authority, by the Ṣūfīs.

46

Patience has three stages: first, it means that the servant ceases to complain, and this is the stage of repentance: second, he becomes satisfied with what is decreed, and this is the rank of the ascetics: third, he comes to love whatever his Lord does with him and this is the stage of the true friends of God. The beginning of asceticism is concern in the soul for the next world and then the coming into existence of the sweetness of hope in God: and concern for the next world does not enter in until concern for this world goes out, nor does the sweetness of hope enter in until the sweetness of desire has departed. True asceticism means the thrusting out from the heart of all thought of worldly things and the reckoning of them as vanity, and only so will asceticism become perfect. Asceticism leads ultimately to fellowship with God. Piety in servants leads on to asceticism and asceticism to love of God and he is not a true ascetic who does not attain to the station of love or the mystic state of fellowship. Love leads to knowledge of the Divine mysteries and those who love abide in God and look to Him only, and He is nearer to them than all else and to them is given a vision of Him unveiled and they see Him with the eye of certainty. Gnosis, truly, is a light which God casts into the heart.

The servant does not attain to assurance of the doctrine of the Unity except by means of gnosis, for gnosis is the light of certainty. Gnosis means the Vision of God, for when the eye of the soul is stripped of all the veils which hindered it from seeing God, then it beholds the reality of the Divine attributes by its own inner light, which goes far beyond the light which is given to perfect faith, for gnosis belongs to a sphere quite other than that of faith.

47

O Light of the heavens and the earth, O Beauty of the heavens and the earth, O Thou Who hast laid the foundations of the heavens and the earth and Who art their Creator, Thou Lord of Majesty and Glory, Thou Who dost bring succour to those who cry unto Thee, Thou Goal of the desire of those who seek, Thou consolation of those who grieve: Thou Who dost give rest to the afflicted, Thou dost answer the cry of those who call upon Thee.

O God, give me light in my heart and light in my tomb, and light in my hearing and light in my sight, and light in my feeling, and light in all my body, and light before me and light behind me. Give me, I pray Thee, light on my right hand and light on my left hand and light above me and light beneath me. O Lord, increase light within me and give me light and illuminate me. These are the lights which the Prophet asked for: verily to possess such light means to be contemplated by the Light of Light.

IBN SĪNĀ (AVICENNA) (428/1037)

Ibn Ṣīnā was of Persian parentage and was born near Bukhārā. He became a great and most original writer: besides other works, he wrote a treatise on his doctrine of Ṣūfism called "The Indications and Annotations" (*al-Ishārāt wa' l-Tanbīhāt*), a doctrine which was based upon the Unity of all Being. He also wrote a "Qaṣīda on the Soul", in which he showed that it is a prisoner in this world.

48

The Beauty of God is shown by His Countenance and His Bounty by what He gives. His Beauty surpasses all other beauty, but it is the veil of His Beauty, and its outward manifestation is linked with its inmost reality. So the revelation of His glory is linked with its concealment, as the sun, if it is lightly veiled, is revealed more plainly, and when it is revealed in its splendour, it is veiled by its own glowing light. Yet the King manifests His glory to His creatures and does not withhold from them the right to meet with Him, but they can only approach Him according to their capacity.

The true interior prayer is the contemplation of God by a pure heart, detached from all worldly desires, concerned not with bodily attitudes, but with the movements of the soul. Such a soul invokes the Supreme Being, for its own perfection, through the contemplation of Him, and for its highest happiness, through its immediate knowledge of Him. Upon such a soul the Divine grace descends, while it is at prayer.

49

Every created thing, by its nature, longs for the perfection which means its well-being, and the perfection of the created being is brought about by the grace of that One Who is essentially perfect. The most perfect object of love is the First Cause of all things: for His Glory is revealed, except to those who are not able to receive the revelation. . He is hidden only from those who are veiled by shortcoming and weakness and defect.

But the gnostics have stripped off the veils of their bodies and have devoted themselves to concern with God . . the soul then has reached the light of the Sun and is able to receive the Divine Illumination when it wills, free from all worldly distractions, until it is wholly sanctified. The gnostic desires God only, none other and adores Him as the only Object worthy of adoration and he is moved not by hope of recompense nor by fear of punishment nor anything else, for his eyes are fixed upon his Lord alone.

There are stages and degrees in the contemplative life, to which the gnostic alone in this world attains. The first step for the gnostic is called Will, which means certainty as to the Way. Through this the gnostic will discipline his soul, through his faith, and will direct it towards God, so that he may attain the joy of union. The second stage is that of self-discipline, which is directed towards three things, removing all save God from the gnostic's choice, subduing his carnal soul to his rational soul, so that the imagination and intellect shall be attracted to the higher things, not the lower, and making the conscience mindful of admonition. The third stage means that the soul, now free from sensual desires, is filled with good thoughts and gives itself up to the spiritual love which seeks to be ruled by the qualities of the Beloved.

Now appear to the gnostic flashes of the Divine Light, like fleeting gleams of lightning, which pass away. By those who experience them, these are called "mystic states" and every state brings joy and becomes more frequent, as the gnostic is more able to receive them. In the fourth stage the mystic sees God in all things, and then in the fifth stage he becomes accustomed to God's Presence, the brief flashes of lightning become a shining flame, and he attains to direct knowledge of God and is continually in fellowship with Him.

Then the gnostic passes on to the stage of contemplating God in Himself: he is absent, yet present, he is departing yet abiding. Then he turns to the world of Reality and his contemplation of God is stable and continuous, and when he passes from striving to attainment, his inmost soul becomes a polished mirror reflecting the Face of God. Then he passes away from himself and contemplates only the Divine Glory and if he looks upon himself, it is only as the one contemplating, and when he has come to this, he has attained complete union with God.

ABŪ SA'ĪD B. ABI'L-KHAYR (440/1048)

Abū Sa'īd b. Abi'l-Khayr was born at Mayhana, in Khurāsān. He was early taught the doctrines of Ṣūfism and became a convert to it. He is known as the author of many mystical quatrains and in his mystical poetry he taught the doctrine of the negation of self as the Way to God and to the abiding life in Him. He was a great teacher and preacher of Ṣūfism and perhaps the first to use to the full the language of imagery for the expression of his beliefs.

50

If men wish to draw near to God, they must seek Him in the hearts of men. They should speak well of all men, whether present or absent, and if they themselves seek to be a light to guide others, then, like the sun, they must show the same face to all. To bring joy to a single heart is better than to build many shrines for worship, and to enslave one soul by kindness is worth more than the setting free of a thousand slaves.

That is the true man of God, who sits in the midst of his fellow-men, and rises up and eats and sleeps and buys and sells and gives and takes in the bazaars amongst other people, and who marries and has social intercourse with other folk, and yet is never for one moment forgetful of God.

51

God, in His purity, looks upon the inmost self (*sirr*) of man and help is given to it from that pure Divine contemplation. This Divine assistance is the guardian of that inmost self, and he who acknowledges the Divine Unity is enabled to do so by that inmost self. It is one of the gifts of God and that gift is made manifest by the favour and mercy of God, not by the merits and acts of man. At first God implanted in man's heart a sense of need and a longing desire and sorrow. Then He looked upon that need and sorrow with favour and pity and placed His gift within the heart and that gift is called the mystic shrine (*sirr*) of God. It is immortal and cannot be destroyed, for it is continually contemplated by God and belongs to Him. It is free from all creatureliness and is only lent to the body. Whoever has that mystic shrine of God is living in truth and whoever has it not, is but an animal.

52

God Almighty has created two fires, one unto life and one unto death: the living fire is the fire of supplication which He has placed in the breasts of His servants in this world, so that their carnal selves may be consumed: that fire burns brightly and when the self is consumed away, suddenly that fire of supplication becomes the fire of longing, and that fire of longing will never die either in this world or the next. This is the flame of which the Apostle spoke when he said: "When God willed good to His servant, He kindled a light in his heart."

It is the vision of the heart that is of value, not the speech of the tongue—the true servant is he who fears the Majesty of God and frees himself from carnal desires. Until you empty yourself of self, you will not be able to escape from it. If you wish that God should dwell in your heart, purify your heart from all save Him, for the

King will not enter a house filled with stores and furniture, He will only enter a heart which is empty of all save Himself and which does not admit yourself with Him.

All the members of your body are filled with doubt and polytheism: you must cast out this polytheism from your heart, so that you may have peace. You cannot believe in God until you deny yourself, that self which keeps you far from God Most High and which says: " So-and-so has done you an injury and such a one has treated you well." All this leads to dependence on creatures and all this is polytheism. The creatures are nothing, the Friend is everything. After this manner it must be known and declared, and having been declared it is necessary to abide by it and in it. To abide by it means that when you have said: " One " you must not again say " Two " and the creature and the Creator are two. The right faith is to say " God ", and therein to stand fast: and to stand fast means that when you have said: " God " you should no more speak of the creatures nor think upon them in your heart, so that it is as if the creatures were not existent. Whatever you see or say, see and say from what is existent, which will never cease to be. Love that One Who, when you shall cease to be, will not Himself cease to be, that you may become one who will never cease to be.

53

God created the souls four thousand years before He created their bodies and placed them near to Himself, and there He shed His Light upon them. He knew how much each soul received as its share from that Light and He bestowed favours on the souls in proportion to the light they received, so that they remained tranquil in that light and became nourished thereby. Those who in this world live in fellowship and agreement with one another, must have been on terms of intimacy there. Here they have friendship with one another and are called the "Friends of God" and they are in that state because they love one another for the sake of God—If one be in the East and another in the West, they find fellowship and comfort in conversing with one another, and although one may belong to an early age and another to a later time, yet the latter finds benefit and comfort only by the speech of the former.

54

Long did we rest e'er yet the arch of the sphere
o'er the void was flung,
Long e'er the azure vaults of the courts of heaven
appeared,
In eternal non-being we slept secure and on us
was stamped
The seal of Thy love, before we had known what
it was to be.

What time the stars and circling spheres of
Heaven were not
While water, air and fire and earth as yet were
not,
The secrets of God's Unity had I revealed
When still my fleshly form and voice and mind
were not.

55

Forth from this world, at Thy bidding, Lord,
most gladly will I go,

What matter the loss or gain to me, if Thou
commandest so.
Nay, for Thy sake, if Thou bidst me, will I cast
me in the Fire,
And my soul itself will I offer, if that be Thy
desire.

Thy Path, wherein we walk, in every step, is fair
Meeting with Thee, whatever way we go, is fair.
Whatever eye doth look upon Thy Face, finds
Beauty there,
Thy Praise, whatever tongue doth give it Thee,
is fair.

When Thy fragrance, by the zephyr, from afar
was borne unto me,
Then my heart to me bade farewell and departed
to seek for Thee ;
Forgotten long since is the body, which once was
its dwelling-place,
Of Thy fragrance has it partaken, one with Thine
Essence to be.

56

The day when the goal was reached and I found
myself with Thee,
The joy of the Blessed ones brought no envy
unto me,
If to Elysian fields, they called me, without
Thyself,
Unto my longing heart, Heaven itself would
straiten'd be.

I said to Him: "For whom dost Thy Beauty
thus unfold?"
He answered me: "For Myself, as I am I was
of old:
For Lover I am and Love and I alone the Beloved,
Mirror and Beauty am I: Me in Myself behold."

The gnostic, who the mystery hath known,
From self set free, now with his Lord is one,
Deny thyself, the Living Truth confess,
Allāh is God, beside Him there is none.

ABU'L-QĀSIM AL-QUSHAYRĪ (465/1074)

Abu'l-Qāsim al-Qushayrī was born at Nīshāpūr. He made a special study of the doctrines of the Ṣūfīs and his "Treatise" (*Risāla*) is a valuable book of reference on Ṣūfism, as he is a reliable and conscientious writer.

57

Gratitude is the vision of the Giver, not of the gift—it comes from God Himself. Hope and fear are like the two wings of a bird, when it is flying straight to its destination: if one wing fails, its flight fails and if both fail, it dies. Hope is the vision of God in His perfect Beauty.

The Divine revelation which comes to those who are waiting in expectation for it, comes like flashes of lightning, then like rays of light and then the light in its full splendour.

O Lightning which flashes forth, from which horizon
of the heavens dost thou shine?
First come the flashes, then the rays, then the full
splendour like a radiant flight,
Manifest only to those who are veiled.

The servant is like a body in the hands of God, plunged in the depths of the ocean of the Unity, having passed away from the self and from the claims of created things, so that at the last the servant returns to what he was at first, before he had begun to be.

ABU'L-ḤASAN AL-JULLĀBĪ AL-HUJWĪRĪ
(469/1079)

Al-Hujwīrī was born at Ghazna, in Afghanistan, and died at Lahore. He travelled a great deal and came into contact with the chief Ṣūfīs and religious leaders of his time and so obtained a knowledge which enabled him to write of the Ṣūfī teaching with great illumination and breadth of outlook. His chief work is "The Unveiling of the Veiled" (*Kashf al-Maḥjūb*), which is the oldest and best-known treatise, in Persian, on Ṣūfism; it sets forth a full account of the Ṣūfī doctrine, including Hujwīrī's own personal views.

58

Know that I have found the universe to be the shrine of the Divine mysteries, for to created things has God entrusted Himself and within that which exists has He hidden Himself. Substances and accidents, elements, bodies, forms and dispositions are all veils of these Mysteries. In the doctrine of the Unity of God, the existence of all these would be polytheism, but God Most High has ordained that this universe, by its own being, should be veiled from His Unity. Therefore, the spirits of men are concerned only with their own phenomenal existence, so that their minds fail to perceive the Divine mysteries, and their spirits but dimly apprehend how wonderfully near to them is God. Man is engrossed with himself and heedless of everything else, and so he fails to recognise the Unity behind all things and is blind to the Beauty of Oneness and will not taste the joy offered to him by the One, and is turned aside by the vanities of this world from the vision of the Truth, and allows the animal soul to predominate, though it is the most potent of all veils between himself and God.

The true sanctuary is the place where contemplation is, and only that one to whom the whole world is the meeting-place where he draws near to God, and a place of retreat where he finds fellowship with Him, knows what it is to be the friend of God. When the veil has been removed, the whole world is his sanctuary, but while he is still veiled, the whole world will remain dark to him, for the darkest of things is the dwelling-place of the Beloved, without the Beloved.

59

Human satisfaction is equanimity under the decrees of Fate, whether it holds or whether it gives, and steadfastness of the soul in regarding passing events, whether they are a manifestation of the Divine Majesty (*jalāl*) or of the Divine Beauty (*jamāl*). It is all the same, to the true servant, whether he is in want or receives bounteously, he remains equally satisfied thereby, and whether he be consumed in the fire of the wrath of the Divine Majesty or whether he be illuminated by the light of the mercy of the Divine Beauty, it is all one to him. Both are manifestations of God and whatever comes from Him is altogether good.

The true mystic, in seeing the act, beholds Him Who acts and since the human being, whatever his qualities, whether he be full of faults or free from them, whether he be veiled or whether he has received illumination from God, belongs to God and was created by Him, to quarrel with the human act, is to quarrel with the Divine Agent.

60

To Him belong Beauty and Majesty and Perfection. His Perfection can be attained only by those who are themselves perfect and whose imperfection has passed away. He whose evidence in gnosis is the Beauty of God, longs continually for the Vision of Him and he whose evidence is the Majesty of God is always hating his own qualities and his heart is filled with awe. Now longing is the result of love, and the hatred of human qualities likewise, since the unveiling of human qualities is due only to love. Therefore faith and gnosis are love and the mark of love is obedience.

Since the Beloved is subsistent, the lover must be annihilated, for the jealousy of the Beloved requires that the subsistence of the lover be annihilated, so that His own dominion be made absolute, and the annihilation of the lover's attributes can only be accomplished by the establishment of the Essence of the Beloved. The lover cannot remain in possession of his own attributes, for in that case he would have no need of the Beauty of the Beloved, but since he knows that he lives by the Beauty of the Beloved, he seeks of necessity to annihilate his own attributes, since by retaining them, he is veiled from the Beloved. So out of love to his Beloved, he becomes an enemy of himself.

61

When the unveiling of the Divine Glory is given to anyone, his existence becomes a burden to him and all his attributes a source of reproach to him : he who belongs to God and to whom God belongs, has no concern with anything else. The real meaning of gnosis is to know that the Kingdom is God's. When anyone knows that all power is in the hand of God, what further concern has he with the creatures, that he should be veiled from God, by himself or them ? All veils come from ignorance; when ignorance has passed away, the veils vanish and this life, by means of gnosis, becomes one with the life to come.

62

When God manifests Himself to the heart of His servant by displaying His Majesty, the servant is filled with awe (*hayba*) and when He manifests Himself to the heart of His servant by displaying His Beauty, he feels the intimacy of fellowship (*uns*). Those who feel awe, because of His Majesty, are troubled, but those who feel fellowship, because of His Beauty, are full of joy. There is a difference between the heart which, from the sight of His Majesty, is consumed in the fire of love, and that heart which, from the sight of His Beauty, is irradiated by the light of contemplation... The power of awe is brought to bear on the carnal soul and its desires, and causes what belongs to human nature to perish, and the power of fellowship is brought to bear on the inmost heart and gives rise to gnosis therein. Therefore God, by the revelation of His Majesty, causes the carnal souls of His lovers to pass away, and by the revelation of His Beauty gives immortality to their hearts.

The terms mortality (*fanā*) and immortality (*baqā*) are applied by the Ṣūfīs to the degree of perfection attained by the saints who have escaped from the pain of conflict and the fetters of the "stations" (*maqāmāt*) and the changes involved in the "states" (*aḥwāl*) and have found what they sought. They have beheld all things that can be seen and have listened to all that can be heard and have come to know the hidden things of the heart; they have realised how imperfect is all that they have discovered, and so they have turned aside from it all and have of set purpose passed away from all desire and are left without desire, and having thus passed away from mortality, they have attained to perfect immortality.

ABŪ ḤĀMID AL-GHAZĀLĪ (505/1111)

al-Ghazālī was born at Ṭūs, in Khurāsān, and early became acquainted with the teachings of Ṣūfism. He gave up a brilliant academic career in order to seek for God only, and found that the way lay in Ṣūfism, and henceforth he consecrated his life to it. Towards the end of his life he established a convent for Ṣūfīs and gave himself up to teaching work and to personal devotion. He is the most famous of all Muslim writers and wrote many treatises on Ṣūfism: the greatest and most complete of these is "The Revivification of Religion" (*Iḥyā 'Ulūm al-Dīn*).

63

All that we behold and perceive by our senses bears undeniable witness to the existence of God and His power and His knowledge and the rest of His attributes, whether these things be manifested or hidden, the stone and the clod, the plants and the trees, the living creatures, the heavens and the earth and the stars, the dry land and the ocean, the fire and the air, substance and accident, and indeed we ourselves are the chief witness to Him ..but just as the bat sees only at night, when the light is veiled by darkness, and cannot therefore see in the daytime, because of the weakness of its sight, which is dazzled by the full light of the sun, so also the human mind is too weak to behold the full glory of the Divine Majesty.

God is One, the Ancient of Days, without prior, Eternal, having no beginning, Everlasting, having no end, continuing for evermore..He is the First and the Last, the transcendent and the immanent, Whose wisdom extendeth over all..He cannot be likened to anything else that exists nor is anything like unto Him, nor is He contained by the earth or the heavens, for He is exalted far above the earth and the dust thereof..The fact of His existence is apprehended by men's reason and He will be seen as He is by that gift of spiritual vision, which He will grant unto the righteous, in the Abode of Eternity, when their beatitude shall be made perfect by the vision of His glorious Countenance.

He is the exalted, Almighty, puissant, Supreme, Who slumbereth not nor sleepeth : neither mortality nor death have dominion over Him. His is the power and the kingdom and the glory and the majesty and to Him belongs creation and the rule over what He has created : He alone is the Giver of life, He is Omniscient, for His knowledge encompasseth all things, from the deepest depths of the earth to the highest heights of the heavens. Not the smallest atom in the earth or the heavens, but is known unto Him, yea, He is aware of how the ants creep upon the hard rock in the darkness of the night : He perceives the movement of the mote in the ether. He beholds the thoughts which pass through the minds of men, and the range of their fancies and the secrets of their hearts, by His knowledge, which was from aforetime. All that is other than Him—men and jinns, angels and Satan, the heavens and the earth, animate beings, plants, inorganic matter, substance and accident, what is intelligible and what is sensible—all were created by His power out of non-existence. He brought them into being, when as yet they had no being, for from eternity He alone existed and there was no other with Him.

64

Yet God, for all His unique Majesty and Greatness, differs from earthly kings, in inspiring His creatures to ask and make their plea to Him, for He says: "Is there any who calls unto Me? I will answer him. Is there any who seeks for forgiveness? I will grant it unto him. Unlike the rulers of the world, He opens the door and lifts the veil and gives leave to His servants to enter into confidential intercourse with Him through prayer. Nor does He limit Himself to giving them leave, but He shows His loving-kindness by inspiring them with the desire for this, and calling them to Him.

Know that your Companion, Who never forsakes you, whether you are at home or abroad, asleep or awake, in life or in death, is your Lord and Master, your Protector and your Creator, and whenever you remember Him, He is there beside you. For God Most High hath said: "I am the Companion of him who remembers Me." Whenever your heart is stricken with grief for your shortcomings in religion, He is there at hand, continually beside you. For He hath said: "I am with those who are contrite in heart, for My sake." If you but knew Him in truth, you would take Him as your Friend and forsake all others but Him. If you are not able to do that at all times, do not fail to set apart time, both night and day, in which you may commune with your Lord and enjoy His Presence in inward converse with Him, and may know what it means to have continual fellowship with God.

65

You ought to know yourself as you really are, so that you may understand of what nature you are and whence you have come to this world and for what purpose you were created and in what your happiness and misery consist. For within you are combined the qualities of the animals and the wild beasts, and also the qualities of the angels, but the spirit is your real essence, and all beside it is, in fact, foreign to you. So strive for knowledge of your origin, so that you may know how to attain to the Divine Presence and the contemplation of the Divine Majesty and Beauty, and deliver yourself from the fetters of lust and passion. For God did not create you to be their captive, but that they should be your thralls, under your control, for the journey which is before you, to be your steed and your weapon, so that you may therewith pursue your happiness, and when you have no more need of them, then cast them under your feet.

66

To be a Ṣūfī means to abide continuously in God and to live at peace with men: whoever abides in God and deals rightly with men, treating them with unfailing kindness, is a Ṣūfī. The right attitude towards your fellow-men is that you should not lay burdens upon them according to your own desire, but rather burden yourself according to their desires. In your dealings with others, treat them as you would wish them to treat you, for the faith of God's servant is not made perfect unless he desires for others what he desires for himself.

The rule of the Ṣūfī is that Poverty should be his adornment and Patience his ornament and Satisfaction his steed and Trust his dignity. God alone is sufficient for him: he employs his members in acts of devotion and it may be that he has no desire at all for worldly things, or if he has, only for what suffices for his needs. His heart is free from defilement and from distraction, because of his love for his Lord, and he looks towards Him in his inmost self, committing all things to Him and having fellowship with Him. He does not rely upon anything, nor does he have fellowship with any, save Him Whom he worships, preferring God to all else.

67

Once I had been a slave: Lust was my master,
Lust then became my servant, I was free:
Leaving the haunts of men, I sought Thy Presence,
Lonely, I found in Thee my company.

Not in the market-place is found the treasure,
Nor by the ignorant, who know not Thee,
Who taunt me, thinking that my search is folly,
But at the end, Thou wilt be found with me.

68

The knowledge which results in renunciation (*zuhd*) consists of the realisation that what is renounced is of little value in comparison with what is received. It is like the knowledge of the merchant who knows that what he receives in exchange for his merchandise is worth more than what he sells, and so he desires the sale: whoever has not the knowledge cannot bring himself to part from his merchandise. So he who has understood that what belongs to God is abiding and that the joys of the other life are better and more lasting than the pleasures of this life, as jewels are better and more durable than snow, desires to exchange this life for that other. No one who possesses snow would find any hardship in exchanging it for jewels and pearls. For this world is like snow exposed to the sun, which continues to melt until it disappears altogether, while the next life is like a precious stone which never passes away.

69

The purpose of music, considered in relation to God, is to arouse longing for Him and passionate love towards Him and to produce states in which He reveals Himself and shows His favour, which are beyond description and are known only by experience, and, by the Ṣūfīs, these states are called 'ecstasy'. The heart's attainment of these states through hearing music is due to the mystic relationship which God has ordained between the rhythm of music and the spirit of man. The human spirit is so affected by that rhythm, that music is the cause to it of longing and joy and sorrow and 'expansion' (*inbisāṭ*) and 'contraction' (*inqibāḍ*), but he who is dull of hearing and unresponsive and hard of heart, is debarred from this joy, and such a one is astonished at the delight of the mystic and his ecstasy—for enjoyment is a kind of apprehension and apprehension requires something to be apprehended and the capacity to apprehend, and he who lacks such a capacity cannot imagine such enjoyment. How can anyone who lacks the sense of taste enjoy food, or he who has lost his hearing, enjoy the pleasure of sweet sounds, or one who is out of his mind enjoy intelligible things? So also, after the sound has reached the ear, the true significance of music is apprehended by the inner sense within the heart, and he who lacks that sense, of necessity takes no pleasure in it.

70

In the invisible world are wonders, in relation to which this visible world is seen to be of no account. He who does not ascend to that world..is but a brute beast: indeed, he is more in error than any brute beast, since the brutes are not given wings wherewith to take flight to that world. Know that the visible world is to the World Invisible as the husk to the kernel, as the outward form and body to the spirit, as darkness to light, and as the ignoble to the sublime. Therefore that invisible world is called the World Supernal and the Spiritual World and the World of Light..He who is in that world above is with God and has the keys of the Unseen.

The window into the unseen is opened in waking hours for the gnostic who has striven and is purified, being delivered from the power of sensual desire. Such a gnostic, sitting in solitude, who closes the channels of the senses, and opens the eye and ear of the spirit, and places his heart in relation with the Divine World, while he says continually: "God, God, God" within his heart, not with his tongue, ceases to be aware of himself, and of this world, and remains seeing only Him Who is Most Glorious and Exalted. Then that window is opened and he sees in his waking moments that which he sees in dreams, and there appear unto him angelic spirits and the prophets and wondrous forms, fair and glorious to behold, and the kingdoms of the heavens and the earth are laid open unto him and he sees what it is not lawful to describe. This gnosis goes far beyond the knowledge of the learned, for it enters the hearts of the prophets and the saints direct from the Creative Truth Himself, nor can it be comprehended except by those who have experience of it.

71

All beauty is loved by the one who is able to perceive beauty, for the perception of beauty is a delight in itself, which is loved for its own sake, not for anything else. Beautiful forms may be loved for themselves and not for any end to be obtained from them, and that cannot be denied: for instance, green things and running water are loved for themselves, not for the sake of drinking the water or eating the green things. So, too, with the blossom and the flowers and the birds, with their fair colours and beautiful forms and their perfectly symmetrical forms, the very sight of them is a joy in itself, and all joy is loved. It cannot be denied that where Beauty is perceived it is natural to love it and if it is certain that God is Beauty, He must be loved by that one to whom His Beauty and His Majesty are revealed. In God and in Him alone are all these causes of love combined and all things lovable found in their highest perfection. For it is to Him that man owes his very existence and the qualities by which he may attain to his perfection. He is the only real Benefactor and the Ultimate Cause of all benefits. If, where beauty is found, it is natural to love it, and if beauty consists in perfection, then it follows that the All-Beautiful, Who is Absolute Perfection, must be loved by those to whom His nature and attributes are revealed.

Finally, man loves God, because of the affinity between the human soul and its Source, for it shares in the Divine nature and attributes, because through knowledge and love it can attain to eternal life and itself become Godlike. Such love, when it has grown strong and overwhelming is called passion (*'ishq*), which has no meaning, but that of love firmly established and limitless. It is reasonable to give this passionate love to that One from Whom all good things are seen to come. In truth, there is nothing good or beautiful or beloved in this world, but comes from His loving-kindness and is the gift of His grace, a draught from the sea of His bounty. For all that is good and fair and lovely in the world, perceived by the intellect and the sight and the hearing and the rest of the senses, from the creation of the world, until it shall pass away, from the summit of the Pleiades unto the ends of the earth, is but a particle from the treasure of His riches and a ray from the splendour of His glory. Is it not reasonable to love Him, Who is thus described, and is it not comprehensible that those who have mystic knowledge of His attributes should love Him more and more until their love passes bounds ? To use the term ' Passion ' for it is indeed wrong in regard to Him, for it fails to express the greatness of their love towards Him.

Glory be to Him, Who is concealed from sight by the brightness of His light. If He had not veiled Himself with Seventy Veils of Light, the splendours of His Countenance would surely consume the eyes of those who contemplate the Beauty which is His.

72

No one who does not know God in this world will see Him in the next and he who does not find the joy of gnosis in this world will not find the joy of vision in the next, since none may make appeal to God in the next world who has not sought His friendship in this world and none may reap who has not sown. A man is raised up only in the state in which he has died, and he dies only in that state in which he has lived, and the only gnosis he takes with him is that wherewith he was blessed in himself, unless it is changed into the Vision of God, face to face, when his joy in it is greatly increased, just as the joy of the lover is doubled when the image of the beloved is exchanged for the reality, for that is the consummation of his joy. For the delights of Paradise are to each one there, only what he desires, and to him who desires only to meet with God Himself, there is no delight save in Him. Indeed, he may suffer thereby, for since the delights of Paradise are only in proportion to his love of God, and his love of God is in proportion to his gnosis, then the origin of spiritual happiness is the gnosis which has been revealed by God through faith.

The delight arising from the Beauty of the Lord is that which the Prophet of God explained when he gave the words of the Lord Most High: "I have prepared for My faithful servants what eye hath not seen nor ear heard and what has not entered into the heart of man" and some of these delights are given beforehand in this world to that one who has wholly purified his heart. The purpose of the gnostics is only to attain to this knowledge and possess it, for it is a consolation unknown to the souls from which it is hidden, and when it is attained, it destroys all anxieties and sensual desires and the heart becomes filled with its grace. Even if the gnostic were cast into the fire, he would not feel it, because of his absorption, and if the delights of Paradise were spread out before him, he would not turn towards them, because of the perfection of the grace that is in him and his perfect attainment, which is above all else that can be attained. How can he who understands only the love of sensible things, believe in the joy of looking upon the Face of God Most High? For such a one there is no vision or form, and what meaning is there for him in the promise of God Most High to His worshippers, and in His statement that He gives the greatest of all joys? But he who knows God knows that all real joys are included in this joy.

73

When the worshipper thinks no longer of his worship or himself, but is altogether absorbed in Him Whom he worships, that state, by the gnostics, is called the passing away of mortality (*fanā'*), when a man has so passed away from himself that he feels nothing of his bodily members, nor of what is passing without, nor what passes within his own mind. He is detached from all that and all that is detached from him: he is journeying first *to* his Lord, then at the end, *in* his Lord. But if during that state, the thought comes to him that he has passed away completely from himself, that is a blemish and a defilement. For perfect absorption means that he is unconscious not only of himself, but of his absorption. For *fanā'* from *fanā'* is the goal of *fanā*. Orthodox theologians may regard these words as meaningless nonsense, but that is not so, for this state of the mystics, in relation to Him Whom they love, is like your state in relation to what you love of position or wealth, or like a human love, when you may be overcome by anger in thinking of a rival, or so engrossed in your beloved, that you perceive nothing else. You do not hear when someone speaks to you, nor see one who passes, though your eyes are open and you are not deaf, for the absorption makes you oblivious of all else and even of the absorption itself. For any attention to the absorption means being diverted from the cause thereof. So having heard the explanation of what is meant by the passing away of mortality (*fanā'*) you should cast aside doubt and cease to deny what you cannot comprehend.

This absorption at first will be like a flash of lightning, lasting but a short time, but then it becomes habitual and a means of enabling the soul to ascend to the world above, where pure and essential Reality is manifested to it, and it takes upon itself the impress of the Invisible World and the Divine Majesty is revealed to it..and at the last, it looks upon God, face to face. When such a mystic returns to this world of unreality and shadows, he regards mankind with pity, because they are deprived of the contemplation of the beauty of that celestial Abode, and he marvels at their contentment with shadows and their attraction to this world of vain deceits. He is present with them in body..but absent in spirit, wondering at their presence, while they wonder at his absence.

74

When the mystic enters into the pure and absolute Unicity of the One and into the Kingdom of the One and Alone, mortals reach the end of their ascent. For there is no ascent beyond it, since ascent involves multiplicity, implying, as it does, an ascent from somewhere and an ascent to somewhere, and when multiplicity has been eliminated, Unity is established and relationship ceases, signs are effaced, there remains neither height nor depth, nor one to descend or ascend. No higher ascent for the soul is possible, for there is no height beyond the highest and no multiplicity in face of the Unity, and since multiplicity has been effaced, no further ascent.

Those who have passed into the unitive life have attained unto a Being transcending all that can be apprehended by sight or insight, for they find Him to transcend in His sanctity all that we have described heretofore. But these can be separated into classes, for some of them, all that can be perceived is consumed away, blotted out, annihilated, but the soul remains contemplating that Supreme Beauty and Holiness and contemplating itself in the beauty which it has acquired by attaining to the Divine Presence, and for such a one, things seen are blotted out, but not the seeing souls. But some pass beyond this and they are the Elect of the Elect, who are consumed by the glory of His exalted Countenance, and the greatness of the Divine Majesty overwhelms them and they are annihilated and they themselves are no more. They no longer contemplate themselves, and there remains only the One, the Real, and the meaning of His Word: "All things perish save His Countenance" is known by experience.

This is the final degree of those who attain, but some of them did not in their ascent follow the gradual process we have described, nor was the ascent long for them. At the very beginning, outstripping their compeers, they attained to a knowledge of the All-Holy and the Divine transcendence. They were overcome at the first by what overcame others at the last. The Divine Epiphany broke in upon them all at once, so that all things perceptible by sight or by insight were consumed by the glory of His Countenance.

Ask that I may be forgiven if my pen has gone astray

or my foot has slipped, for to plunge into the abyss of the Divine mysteries is a perilous thing and no easy task is it to seek to discover the Unclouded Glory which lies behind the veil.

75

It is for the saint to descend from the mountain of transfiguration to the lower levels of this world, so that the weak may seek out his company and may kindle their lights at the radiance which the saint has brought from the heavenly places, just as bats find their light in what remains of the sunlight and are content with the light of the stars in the watches of the night and thereby live a life suited to their bodily state, though not the life of those who come and go in the full light of the sun. The saint is one whose eyes are open, so that he sees clearly and needs none to lead him, but it is his business to lead the blind or those weak of sight, for his relation to the weaker brethren is that of one who walks on water to those who walk on land. Some may learn to swim, but to walk on water is only given to those who have reached spiritual perfection. It is the glory of the saint to spend himself for those in need and to undertake the task of shepherding them into Paradise. Again, it is the mark of saintship to show compassion to all God's servants, to be pitiful towards them, and to fight for them, and with them, against the forces of evil.

76

Praise be to God, Who hath freed the hearts of His saints from any inclination to the vanities of this world and its glamour and hath purified their inmost selves from the contemplation of anything but His Majesty.

These are they whom He hath chosen for Himself that they might be devoted to the proclamation of His glory, to whom He hath revealed His Names and His Attributes, until they were illumined by the radiance of their knowledge of Him. To them hath He unveiled the Splendour of His Countenance until they were consumed by the fire of His love.

He hath taken captive their thoughts and their spirits by longing to meet with Him and to look upon Him, and hath fixed their sight and their insight upon the Vision of the Beauty of His Presence, until by the inbreathing of the spirit of union, they have become rapt beyond themselves..and they see nothing like unto Him among things visible or invisible and they are mindful of nothing in the two worlds save Him alone. If any form present itself to their outward gaze, their inward vision passes beyond it to Him Who formed it: if sweet music breaks in upon their hearing, their inmost thoughts pass from it to the Beloved. If any sound reaches them, which is disquieting or disturbing or affecting or giving rise to joy or sorrow or making for merriment or for longing or stirring up to excitement—they are disturbed only for His sake, their joy is in Him alone, and they are disquieted only on His account..Their longing is only for that which is to be found in His Presence and their going to and fro is round about Him alone. For from Him is all that they hear and it is to Him that they give heed, since He hath closed their eyes to all but Him and hath made them deaf to all words save His. These are they whom God hath called to be His saints, who are His and His alone.

ABU'L-MAJDŪD B. ĀDAM SANĀ'Ī (545/1150)

Sanā'ī was born at Ghazna and was attached to the court of Bahrām Shāh. He made a thorough study of Ṣūfism and was one of the great mystical poets of Persia. Of him Rūmī, a still greater Ṣūfī poet, wrote:

'Aṭṭār was the spirit and Sanā'ī the two eyes,
We follow after Sanā'ī and 'Aṭṭār.

While still quite young Sanā'ī renounced the world and adopted the religious life. He wrote a considerable number of poems, the most famous being " The Garden of Truth " (*Ḥadīqat al-Ḥaqīqat*).

77

God is the Self-Existent..consisting of none but Himself: His acts and His Essence are beyond instrument and direction, for His Being is above " Be " and " He " ..He is the only Real Existent: all other existences exist only in the imagination and are subject to His existence. He is the Maker of our outward forms and also He discerns the images of our inmost heart. He is the Creator of the existent and the non-existent, the Maker of the hand and what it holds..He made Intelligence which proclaims His power: He made matter capable of receiving form..He is the origin and the root of material things..the Giver of every good gift, of gratitude and the grateful. He is the Source of all Creation, and to Him it all returns. All come from Him and all returns to Him..all are His, all seek Him; the motion of light is towards light, for how can light be separated from the Sun? No mind can attain to a knowledge of the Absolute God: the reason and the soul cannot know His Perfection, the mind is dazzled by His Majesty, the eye of the soul is blinded by His perfect

Beauty. The imagination is incapable of realising the glory of His Essence: the understanding is unable to interpret His Nature and its mode of being. The soul is but a servant in His train and reason a pupil in His school. What is reason in this temporal world? Only one who writes crookedly the script of God.

78

Wheresoever you will incline, let it be in accordance with the Divine Spirit within you: do not incline in opposition to it, but soar above the snares of earth, reaching the dwelling-place of the Most High, regarding the borders of the world of spirit with the eye of your Divine being. Abandon vain conceits so that you may find admission to the Court of God, for that mansion of eternity is prepared for you and this temporal world is not your true home—abandon to-day and sacrifice your life for the sake of to-morrow. . Arise and leave this base world in order that you may find the One and Only God. Leave behind your body and your life and reason and faith and in His Path find for yourself a soul. If you wish to possess a pearl, O man, leave the desert and walk beside the sea. Strive in the road of God, O soldier: if you are without ambition, you will have no honour, but the man who despises his own body shall ride up on the air like fire. He who through love to God, is like a candle in the Path, like a candle shall be crowned with fire.

79

The high road to God for your spirit, by which your prayers can reach God, is the polishing of the mirror of the heart. The mirror will not become purified from the rust of infidelity and hypocrisy by rebellion and opposition.

The mirror is polished by your unwavering faith and your perfect sincerity in religion. Do not confuse the Image with the mirror, they are not the same: the mirror reflects the image by means of the light and the light cannot be separated from the Sun: if, then, the light is not reflected, the fault lies in the mirror. Whosoever remains veiled is like the owl and the sun. If the owl cannot see in the sunlight, it is because of its own weakness, not because of the sun. The light of the sun shines throughout the world; the misfortune comes from the weakness of the night-bird's eye. He speaks foolishly who does not know that God manifests Himself by His indwelling in man. If you wish that the mirror should reflect the face, you must hold it straight and keep it bright. Break loose from the chain with which you have fettered yourself, for you will be free when you have got clear of earthly fetters. Whatever increases the brightness of your heart, brings nearer God's manifestation of Himself to you.

80

Love knows that renunciation is the key of the gate: in the crucible of renunciation the lover is prepared to consume all that keeps him from the Beloved. To the lovers in the soul-inflaming Path, no outward glory is to be compared with the secret fire within. He whose soul is aflame for the Path does not lag behind at the halting-place. In that world where love tells the secret, "thou" no longer exists and reason no longer continues: lovers are beside themselves in the Presence of the Beloved. When they urge on the steed of their hearts towards Him, they cast all things away at His feet: they throw down life and heart before Him and join themselves to Him. For them all is nothing, He alone is..O you who love the Beauty of the Presence of the Invisible, until you seek to contemplate His Face, you will never drink the draught of communion with Him, nor taste the delight of inward converse with Him. When He admits you to His court, ask from Him nothing but Himself. When your Lord has chosen you as His lover, your eye has seen all things: the world of Love allows of no duality—what talk is this of "me" and "you"? When you come forth from life and your dwelling-place, then through God you will see God.

'ABD AL-QĀDIR JĪLĀNĪ (561/1166)

'Abd al-Qādir Jīlānī is regarded as the patron saint of Baghdad, and was the founder of the Qādiriyya Order. He studied Ṣūfism in Baghdad and then spent long years in asceticism and self-discipline, until he attained to the mystical experience and the life of the saints. He was responsible for a large number of writings.

81

There are two classes of true believers. First, those who seek a master in the Way that leads to the Majesty of God, who may act as an intermediary between them and God, so they do not accept as evidence of the right way, anything in which they do not see the footstep of the Prophet before them. The second class are those who, when they seek to tread the right Path do not see before them the footprint of any of God's creatures, for they have removed all thought of what He has created from their hearts and concern themselves solely with God.

82

Die, then, to the creatures, by God's leave, and to your passions, by His command, and you will then be worthy to be the dwelling-place of the knowledge of God. The sign of your death to the creatures is that you detach yourself from them and do not look for anything from them. The sign that you have died to your passions is that you no longer seek benefit for yourself, or to ward off injury, and you are not concerned about yourself, for you have committed all things unto God. The sign that your will has been merged in the Divine Will is that you seek nothing of yourself or for yourself—God's Will is working in you. Give yourself up into the hands of God, like the ball of the polo-player, who sends it to and fro with his mallet, or like the dead body in the hands of the one who washes it, or like the child in its mother's bosom.

SHIHĀB AL-DĪN SUHRAWARDĪ ḤALABĪ AL-MAQTŪL (587/1191)

Suhrawardī Ḥalabī studied in Baghdad, and called himself "The Seeker of the Invisible World" (*al-Murīd bi'l-Malakūt*). When he had become an adept in the Ṣūfī Path, he settled down in Aleppo and there lived the life of a Ṣūfī philosopher. He was accused of heresy and Saladin ordered that he should be put to death. He wrote a number of books setting forth his doctrine of Illumination, the most important of which were "The Philosophy of Illumination" (*Ḥikmat al-Ishrāq*) and "The Temples of Light" (*Hayākil al-Nūr*).

83

O my God, Thou Lord of all that exists, of all intellectual beings and all sensible things, Thou Giver of minds and souls, Who hast laid the foundations of the world, First Cause of all existence and Dispenser of all bounty, Thou Maker of hearts and spirits and Fashioner of forms and bodies, O Light of lights and Ruler of all the sphere, Thou art the First, there was none before Thee; Thou art the Last, there shall be none after Thee. The angels are not able to comprehend Thy Majesty and men cannot attain to a knowledge of the perfection of Thine Essence. O God, set us free from the fetters of this world and of the flesh, and deliver us from all evil that may hinder us. Send down upon our spirits Thy gracious influence and shed forth upon our souls the bright beams of Thy Light. The mind of man is but one drop in the ocean of Thy Kingdom and the soul is but a spark of Thy Divine Glory.

Praise be to Him Whom the sight cannot perceive, nor can the thought conceive of His likeness: to Thee be thanksgiving and praise. Thou dost give and Thou dost take away: Thou art the All-Bountiful and the All-Abiding. Praise be to Him, for His is the power over all things and unto Him shall ye return.

84

The essence of the First Absolute Light, God, gives constant illumination, whereby it is manifested and it brings all things into existence, giving life to them by its rays. Everything in the world is derived from the Light of His Essence and all beauty and perfection are the gift of His bounty, and to attain fully to this illumination is salvation.

From the stage of " I " the seeker passes to the stage of " I am not " and " Thou art ", and then to the stage of " I am not and Thou art not ", for he is now himself one with the One. The vision of God and the reception of His Light mean unification (*ittiṣāl*) and union (*ittiḥād*) with His Essence, Who is the Light of lights.

FARĪD AL-DĪN'AṬṬĀR (626/1229)

Farīd al-Dīn 'Aṭṭār was born near Nīshāpūr, a place famous as a centre of Ṣūfī mysticism. It was while he was engaged in his work as a druggist (*'aṭṭār*) that the call came to him to follow the religious life. He travelled far and wide and for thirty-nine years occupied himself in studying the teaching and sayings of the Ṣūfī saints. Then he went into complete seclusion and became absorbed in the contemplation of the Divine Essence. He spent most of his long life in literary work and wrote " The Memoirs of the Saints " (*Tadhkirat al-Awliyā*) and many poems on mystical subjects.

85

A Ṣūfī devotee began to weep in the middle of the night and said : " This is what I see the world to be : it is like a closed casket in which we are placed and in which, through our ignorance, we spend our time in folly. When Death opens the lid of the casket, each one who has wings takes his flight to Eternity, but that one who is without wings, remains in the casket, a prey to a thousand afflictions. Then give the wing of the mystic sense to the bird of spiritual desire : give a heart to reason, and ecstasy to the soul. Before the lid is taken away from this casket become a bird of the Way to God and develop your wings and your feathers. Nay, rather, burn your wings and your feathers and destroy yourself by fire, and so will you arrive at the Goal before all others.

86

The lover thinks nothing of his own life, for he who is a lover, whether he be an ascetic or a libertine, is prepared to sacrifice his life for the sake of love. If your spirit is at enmity with your soul, sacrifice your soul and you will be able to go on your way unhindered. If your soul is a distraction to you on the road, cast it aside, then look straight before you and give yourself to contemplation. If you are bidden to renounce your faith or to give up your life, cast away both: abandon your faith and sacrifice your life. If one who is ignorant of spiritual things should say that it is untrue that Love should be preferred to infidelity or faith, say to him: "What has Love to do with infidelity or faith?" Do lovers concern themselves with their souls? A lover sets fire to the whole harvest: he puts the knife to his own throat and pierces his own body. Torment and affliction are what pertain to Love. He who has his feet set firmly in the abode of Love renounces at once both infidelity and faith.

87

The Phœnix is a wonderful bird, which is found in Hindustān. It has no mate, but dwells alone in solitude. Its beak is wonderfully hard and long, like a flute, containing holes to the number of nearly a hundred. Each of these holes gives forth a different tone and each tone reveals a different mystery. The art of music was taught to this bird by a philosopher, who became its friend. When the Phœnix utters these sounds, bird and fish are agitated thereby: all the wild beasts are reduced to silence and, by that entrancing music, are bereft of their senses.

The Phœnix lives about a thousand years: it knows quite clearly the time of its death and when this knowledge is tearing at its heart, it gathers fuel, a hundred trees or more and heaps them up in one spot. It hastens to place itself in the midst of the pyre and utters a hundred laments over itself. Then through each of those holes in its beak, it gives forth plaintive cries of woe, out of the depths of its spotless soul, and as it utters its dying lament, it trembles like a leaf. At the sound of its music, all the birds of the air gather together, and the wild beasts come, attracted by the sound, and all assemble to be present at the death of the Phœnix, knowing that they must die like it. When the moment has come to draw its last breath, the Phœnix spreads out its tail and its feathers and thereby a fire is kindled and the flames spread swiftly to the heaped-up wood and it blazes up with vigour. Soon both pyre and bird become a glowing red-hot mass. When the glowing charcoal is reduced to ashes and but one spark remains, then, from the ashes, a new Phœnix arises into life.

88

One night, the moths gathered together, tormented by the longing to unite themselves with the candle. They all said: "We must find someone to give us news of that for which we long so earnestly."

One of the moths then went to a castle afar off and saw the light of a candle within. He returned and told the others what he had seen and began to describe the candle as intelligently as he could. But the wise moth, who was the chief of their assembly, said: "He has no real information to give us about the candle." Another moth then visited the candle and passed close to the light, drawing near to it and touching the flames of that which he desired, with his wings: the heat of the candle drove him back and he was vanquished. He, too, came back and revealed something of the mystery, explaining something of what union with the candle meant, but the wise moth said to him: "Your explanation is really worth no more than your comrade's was."

A third moth rose up, intoxicated with love, and threw himself violently into the candle's flame. He hurled himself forward and stretched out his antennæ towards the fire. As he entered completely into its embrace, his members became glowing red like the flame itself. When the wise moth saw from afar that the candle had identified the moth with itself and had given the moth its own light, he said: "This moth has fulfilled his desire, but he alone understands that to which he has attained. None other knows it and that is all."

In truth, it is the one who has lost all knowledge and all trace of his own existence who has, at the same time, found knowledge of the Beloved. So long as you will not ignore your own body and soul, how will you ever know the Object you love?

89

If you are possessed of discernment joined with knowledge, seek the company of the dervishes and become one with them: associate with none but them. Love for the dervishes is the key which opens the door into Paradise and those who hate them are worthy of anathema. The dervish's garment is nothing but a patched robe, and he is not led astray by creaturely desires and passions. Until a man treads his carnal self underfoot, how can he find the way to the abode of God Most High? The man who walks in the Path of God has no longing after fine palaces and fair gardens: in his heart is nothing but the pain of yearning love.

Though you raise your palace as high as the heavens, yet in the end you will come to be buried under the earth, and though your strength and power were like those of Rustam, yet at last you will die like Bahrām, and be brought down to the tomb. Be not unmindful of Eternity and set not your heart upon the transient goods of this world. Be patient in the midst of the tribulations of this life and when things go well, give thanks to God Almighty.

90

O you who wander wilfully away from the true Path, know that he who desires the palace of the King, which is more desirable than any palace here, has but to draw near to it. It is the habitation of the soul, which abides for ever; it is the goal of our desires, the resting-place of the heart, the seat of Truth itself. The Presence of God Most High is as a mighty Ocean and the Gardens of Paradise, with all their joys, are but as the least drop in it. He Who possesses the Ocean, possesses the drop also. All that is not the Ocean is mere vanity. Since you can find the way to the Ocean itself, why do you hasten to seek a single drop of dew? Can the one who shares in the secrets of the Sun dally with a mote in its beams? When a man has become one with the Whole, what concern has he with the part? What need of the members of his body, has one who has found his soul?

If you, O man, have found your reality to be one with the Whole, then contemplate the Whole, seek out the Whole, become one with the Whole and choose for yourself the Whole.

91

The whole world is a market-place for Love,
For naught that is, from Love remains remote.
The Eternal Wisdom made all things in Love:
On Love they all depend, to Love all turn.
The earth, the heavens, the sun, the moon, the stars
The centre of their orbit find in Love.
By love are all bewildered, stupefied,
Intoxicated by the Wine of Love.
From each, a mystic silence Love demands,
What do all seek so earnestly? 'Tis Love.
Love is the subject of their inmost thoughts,
In Love no longer "Thou" and "I" exist,
For self has passed away in the Beloved.
Now will I draw aside the veil from Love,
And in the temple of mine inmost soul
Behold the Friend, Incomparable Love,
He who would know the secret of both worlds
Will find the secret of them both, is Love.

92

The Valley of Gnosis has neither beginning nor end. No other road is like the road which is hidden therein, nor any road there like any other road there, but the traveller in the body is other than the traveller in the spirit. Soul and body are for ever in a state of deficiency or perfection according to their strength and weakness. Therefore, of necessity, the road is revealed to each one according to his capacity for that revelation. On this road, trodden by Abraham, the friend of God, how could the feeble spider be a companion to the elephant? The progress of each will be in accordance with his spiritual state. Though the gnat were to fly with all its might, could it ever equal the perfection of the wind? Since, then, there are different ways of making the journey, no two birds will fly alike. Each finds a way of his own, on this road of mystic knowledge, one by means of the *Miḥrāb* and another through the idols. When the Sun of Gnosis shines forth from the heaven above, on to this most blessed road, each is enlightened according to his capacity and finds his own place in the knowledge of the Truth.

When that sun shines upon him, the dustbin of this world is changed for him into a rose-garden: the kernel is seen beneath the rind. No longer does the lover see any particle of himself, he sees only the Beloved: wheresoever he looks, he sees always His Face, in every atom he beholds His dwelling-place. A hundred thousand mysteries are revealed to him from under the veil, as clearly as the sun. Yet thousands of men are lost eternally, for one who perfectly apprehends these mysteries. He must be perfect, who would succeed in this quest, who would plunge into this fathomless sea. If the joy of its secrets be revealed to him, every moment will renew his longing for it..

Even if you should attain to the Throne of Glory, do not cease each moment to say: "Is there more than this?" Plunge yourself into the Sea of Gnosis, or if you cannot do that, sprinkle the dust of the road upon your head. O you who remain asleep—and it is no matter for congratulation—why do you not put on mourning?

If you have not attained to the joy of union with the Beloved, at least arise and put on signs of mourning for your separation from Him. If you have not looked upon the Beauty of the Beloved, arouse yourself, do not sit still, but seek out those mysteries destined for you, and if as yet you do not know them, seek them out in shame.

93

Strive to acquire the mystic gnosis, so that you may learn to know God. He who truly knows God by contemplation, realises that Eternal Life means passing away from the personal self. Without this knowledge man has no real existence: he is not worthy to approach God, nor will he attain to the goal of his desires. If you really know your self and its desires, you will know God Most High and His gifts.

He alone is the true gnostic who knows God, and whoever is without this knowledge is unfit to be counted among human beings. The gnostic has a heart full of sincere and constant love, all his actions are pure and without stain. The one to whom the gift of gnosis has been given finds no place in his heart save for God alone.

To the gnostic, this world is of no concern, nay, more, he gives no thought to himself. Gnosis means that the gnostic passes away from himself into God. How can the one who does not completely pass away from self attain to this perfection? The gnostic is occupied neither with this world nor the next: he is not concerned with any but his Lord. Because he has died altogether to himself, he is completely absorbed in the attainment of union with God.

94

Thou art fire, but Thy fire is veiled, for in all to which Thou hast joined Thyself, Thou art under a veil. Thou art the Breath of Life in both body and soul. Thou art the Water of Life to be found in every place. In every form Thou dost manifest Thyself, according to Thy will; even in the dust are Thy mysteries shown forth; Thou art the mine and dost show Thyself in its jewels. Thou, the Creator, art seen in the creatures, Spirit shining through gross matter.

Thou art God in Absolute Unity and Thou dwellest here in body and soul, for Thou art the Divine Essence dwelling in the midst of each one of us. O Lord Most High, how glorious is the manifestation of Thy Light! Thou art the Sought and the Seeker: what remains to be said? Give me, I pray Thee, to drink from the cup of Immortality, for Thou art the Cup and the Wine and Cup-bearer.

Since I am myself part of the Mystery of the Unity, happy will be that moment when soul shall be free from body and return unto its Home.

95

In the deep waters of the ocean of annihilation I would seek to be, for though I aspire to the Sun, yet, since one is powerless to attain to Thy great height, I would aspire to sleep at Thy feet. Behold what grief I suffer without Thee! But now, since I have become nothing, I know that in the end I shall attain again to my desire. I said unto Thee: "I have passed away, as I was asked to do." Thou saidst unto me: "I will bring thee unto Eternal Life, as thou hast wished, for when thou dost see thyself as nothing, then will I give unto thee such an existence as thou hast desired."

Every moment now I spend in loving adoration of Another than myself. Long ago I died to mine own existence and if now I live, it is in the existence of Another. I sacrificed all tranquillity and ease and renounced all hope of fame, so that I might attain to complete annihilation. I laid down my life and sacrificed my soul, and all mankind became as nothing to me. Now I have arisen, and I am free from all grief of soul, for I am set free from the world of Existence and Non-Existence and I dwell beyond both. I have taken my flight from phenomenal existence to non-entity.

I am without body and soul and surely these are necessary to me. Without these, what am I? I am that which I was meant to be. Within myself, I have no knowledge of myself, for self-less I was meant to be. Happy is the one who has thus passed away from mortality, for passing away is the essence of abiding in immortality. This I know, that self-annihilation is a glorious thing, but that which I do not know is what I am yet to be.

96

For you there is an ascent of the soul towards the Divine Light, therefore shall your heart and soul in the end attain to union with that Light. With your whole heart and soul, seek to regain Reality, nay, seek for Reality within your own heart, for Reality, in truth, is hidden within you. The heart is the dwelling-place of that which is the Essence of the universe, within the heart and soul is the very Essence of God. Like the saints, make a journey into your self; like the lovers of God, cast one glance within. As a lover now, in contemplation of the

Beloved, be unveiled within and behold the Essence. Form is a veil to you and your heart is a veil. When the veil vanishes, you will become all light.

Tear aside the veils of all you see in this world and you will find yourself apart in solitude with God. If you draw aside the veils of the stars and the spheres, you will see that all is one with the Essence of your own pure soul. If you will but tear aside the veil, you will become pure, as He is pure. Cast aside the veil from existence and non-existence and you will see forthwith the true meaning of God's purpose. When you have cast aside the veil, you will see the Essence and all things will be shown forth within the Essence. If you draw aside the veil from the Face of the Beloved, all that is hidden will be made manifest and you will become one with God, for then will you be the very Essence of the Divine.

97

Save Thee, I see nought in the two worlds, for in truth Thou alone dost exist in this world and in that. From everlasting Thou wast and changeless shalt be: unto eternity is Thy Being and shall be for ever. O Thou Who didst make manifest both time and place, Thou hast created both the soul of man and the universe wherein he dwells, and Thou dost cause the spheres to revolve and dost make the hearts of thousands to be filled with awe and amazement at Thy manifestation of Thyself.

Now I am made one with Thee and from that Union my heart is consumed with rapture and my tongue is all bewildered. By union, I have been merged in the Unity, I am become altogether apart from all else. I am Thou and Thou art I—nay, not I, all is altogether Thou.

I have passed away, " I " and " Thou " no more exist. We have become one and I have become altogether Thou.

By union with Thee, I have become the perfected gnostic and now the gnostic has vanished away and I have become altogether the Creative Truth. I am free from both pride and passion and desire. I reveal the Divine Mysteries and thereby I fill the lovers of God throughout the world with amazement and a hundred thousand creatures remain astonished at me. All forms are consumed in the flames, when the candle of Union with Him is set alight and blazes up.

When the paintings are hidden, thou wilt see the Painter.

O brother, I will tell you the mystery of mysteries. Know, then, that painting and Painter are one! When your faith is made perfect, you will never see yourself, save in Him.

SHIHĀB AL-DĪN ABŪ ḤAFS AL-SUHRAWARDĪ
(632/1234)

Shihāb al-Dīn al-Suhrawardī was a Persian by birth, but lived in Baghdad. He was the founder of the Ṣūfī order of the Suhrawardiyya, found chiefly in Persia and India. He represents the pantheistic development of Ṣūfism. He was famed as a spiritual director and was the author of " The Gifts of Divine Knowledge " (*'Awārif al-Ma'ārif*).

98

The purpose of Retreat (*khalwa*) is to draw near to God, and the heart is filled with joy..and the filling of the heart with light strengthens the attractive force of the Spirit of God, which draws it—the heart—to its true abiding place, the Invisible World, where it is perfectly tranquillised and, like a polished mirror, it reflects the Divine radiance. This attraction is stronger than that of the magnet to the iron. As the magnet attracts the iron because of their affinity in substance, so there is an affinity between the Divine and the human spirit, which draws them together.

Retreat is like a smith's forge in which, by the fire of austerity, the desire becomes fused, purified, delicate and gleaming like a mirror and in it appeareth the form of the Invisible. For every morning of the retreat, a veil should lift and the retreatant find himself drawing ever nearer to God, so that in forty mornings, the forty-fold veil should be lifted and the purified human nature should return from a land that is far-off to the land of proximity, and the vision of the splendour of Eternity without beginning, should be made certain for it and be manifested to it.

99

The spiritual director so teaches that he makes God to be loved by His servants and makes the servants of God to be loved by Him. He leads the novice along the road of purification, and when the soul is purified, the mirror of the heart is polished and there is reflected in it the splendour of the Divine Glory, and there shines within it the radiance of the Divine Beauty, and the insight is rapt away to contemplation of the splendour of the Eternal Majesty and the vision of the Everlasting Perfection. Then the servant cannot but love his Lord, and that is the fruit of purification. The mirror of the heart also, when it is polished, reflects this world and all it contains, and the world to come and all its treasures, and to the inner sight is revealed the reality of the two worlds. Then the servant attains to the Two Abodes and he desires what is abiding and renounces what is transient. It is the work of the spiritual director to help towards this purification.

100

Music does not give rise, in the heart, to anything which is not already there: so he whose inner self is attached to anything else than God is stirred by music to sensual desire, but the one who is inwardly attached to the love of God is moved, by hearing music, to do His will. What is false is veiled by the veil of self and what is true by the veil of the heart and the veil of the self is a dark, earthly veil, and the veil of the heart is a radiant, heavenly veil.

The common folk listen to music according to nature, and the novices listen with desire and awe, while the listening of the saints brings them a vision of the Divine gifts and graces, and these are the gnostics to whom listening means contemplation. But finally, there is the listening of the spiritually perfect, to whom, through music, God reveals Himself unveiled.

101

When the pure in heart utter the *takbīr* (God is Most Great) as they begin their prayer, they enter into the heavenly places and are kept from Satanic distractions ..The hearts of those who seek to draw near to God, come nearer and nearer and ascend through the heavenly spheres, and with each sphere to which they ascend, they leave behind them something of the darkness of self, until they pass beyond the heavens and stand before the

Throne of God, and then all thought of self passes away in the radiant light of the Divine Majesty and the darkness of the self disappears in the light of the heart, just as the darkness of night vanishes in the light of day.

102

Those who have attained the final stage of the way—"confirmation" (*tamkīn*), have left the mystic states (*aḥwāl*) behind them and have pierced the veils and their spirits dwell in Essential Light. They enjoy the fellowship (*uns*) which is the rejoicing of the spirit in the perfection of the Divine Beauty..Some ascend to the stage which means the inward possession of the light of certainty (*anwār al-yaqīn*) and the contemplation of the Invisible, being rapt away in contemplation from their own existences and this means the manifestation of the Essence, to the elect, and this station is a stage in union. Above this is certain knowledge (*ḥaqq al-yaqīn*)—the annihilation point of lovers, when the servant is wholly filled with the light of contemplation—spirit, heart and soul, until he is transformed, and this is the highest degree of union.

'UMAR IBN AL-FĀRIḌ (632/1235)

Ibn al-Fārīḍ was born in Cairo and was early converted to Ṣūfism. He used to spend long periods in seclusion and meditation in the Muqattam Hills, near Cairo. Being told that his time of illumination was near and he should go to Mecca to receive it, he went there and remained for fifteen years. Then he returned to Cairo, where he was accepted by the people as a saint. He is the greatest of Arab mystical poets and left one volume of poetry, his *Dīwān*, a collection of odes which are mainly mystical. To him God was Absolute Beauty and it is with this aspect of the Divine Nature that he is chiefly concerned.

103

Though He be hidden from me, yet by each of my members He is seen, in every lovely thing, that is fair and gives joy to the heart: in the lute's sweet note and the melodious reed, when they are mingled in harmonious notes. He is seen in rich pastures where the gazelles are found among the thickets, in the coolness of the evening, or in the morning, at the dawn. He is seen, too, in the trailing skirts of the zephyr, when it brings to me its fragrant balm, and when I suck wine-drops in a shady spot, as kisses from the goblet's lip.

The darkness has now, through Thee, become bright, since Thou hast given me guidance from Thy Radiant Light. When Thou wast gone, in outward manifestation, from my sight, I looked within me and there I found Thee..That my outward self should shine forth is not wonderful when mine inward is Thy dwelling-place.

104

You see the forms of things revealed to you, in every place, from behind the veil. He has joined all that appears in them, by His wisdom, and their forms appear to you in many different kinds. They were silent and now they speak; they were at rest and now they move; they had no light and now they give forth radiance.

In a single moment, consider all that is before you, for it will not stay for long. For all you see is the work of One Who is alone, but He is hidden by a veil. If He removes the veil, you will see none but Him, and no doubts will remain, nor outer forms, which caused the doubt. You know, most surely, with that unveiling, that it is by His light, that you are guided, in the gloom, to His actions.

105

Let my passionate love for Thee overwhelm me and have pity on the blazing flames of my heart's love for Thee. If I ask to see Thee unveiled, bestow on me that which I ask and answer me not: "Thou shalt not see Me." O heart, thou hast promised me to have patience in thy love, beware, then, of being straitened and wearied. Love is life itself, and to die of love will give the right to be forgiven.

Say to those who went before me and those who will come after me and to those who are with me now, who have seen my grief, "Learn from me and follow in my steps: listen to me and tell of my passion among mankind."

I have been alone with the Beloved and we shared secrets which meant more than the breeze when night comes. Then the Vision I had hoped for was revealed to my sight, and made me known to men, when I had been unknown. The sight of His beauty and His Majesty bewildered me and in my ecstasy, my tongue could no more speak. Look upon the fairness of His Face and you will find all beauty pictured in it and if all beauty were found in a face and it seemed perfect, beholding Him, it would say: "There is no God but He and He is Most Great."

MUḤYĪ AL-DĪN IBN AL-'ARABĪ (638/1240)

Ibn al-'Arabī was born at Murcia, in Spain. He studied Ṣūfism first in Seville and then travelled to Egypt, Syria,

Baghdad and Asia Minor, settling finally in Damascus, where he died. He was a great pantheistic mystic and a very original thinker, who made use of many systems of thought, including Hellenism. He was one who believed that he had the illumination of the Divine Light within himself and in that light he felt that he could see the mysteries of the Unseen, made manifest. His many works include "The Meccan Revelations" (*al-Futūḥāt al-Makkiyya*), "The Bezels of Divine Wisdom" (*Fuṣūṣ al-Ḥikam*), "The Book of Answers" (*Kitāb al-Ajwiba*) and "The Interpretation of Divine Love" (*Tarjumān al-Ashwāq*).

106

Within my heart, all forms may find a place,
The cloisters of the monk, the idol's fane
A pasture for gazelles, the Sacred House
Of God, to which all Muslims turn their face:
The tables of the Jewish Law, the Word
Of God, revealed unto His Prophet true.
Love is the faith I hold, and whereso'er
His camels turn, the one true faith is there.

107

The veils of darkness and light, by which God is veiled from the world, are only what describes the contingent, because it is in the midst and it looks only to itself and it does not look to what is within the veil. If the veils were raised from the contingent the contingency would be revealed and the necessary and the imaginable, because the veil is raised, but the veils continue to be a concealment, and it must be so. Consider this world in regard to the raising of the veil, for He spoke of consuming, by the glory of His countenance, the creature who apprehends it and sometimes He says of Himself that the creatures can see Him and not be consumed, declaring that the veils are raised in the Vision, and the Vision itself is a veil. "The eye of His creature does not see Him," and if men understood the meaning of this, they would know themselves, and if they knew themselves, they would know God: and if they really knew God, they would be satisfied with Him and would think about Him alone, not about the kingdom of the heavens and the earth. If, indeed, they knew the truth of the matter, they would realise that He is Himself the Essence of the kingdom of the heavens and the earth.

If it were not for the Light, nothing at all could be apprehended by the mind or the senses or the imagination, and the name given to the light, varies with the faculties, which we also call by different names. According to the common folk, the name is given to the mind, and among the gnostics, to the light of perception; when you apprehend what is audible, you call the light which apprehends, hearing, and when you apprehend what is visible, you call the light seeing. Light involves a relationship, for apprehending what is apparent. Everyone who perceives must have some relationship to the light, by which he is made able to perceive, and everything which is perceived has a relationship with God, Who is Light, that is, all which perceives and all which is perceived.

108

He is and there is with Him no before or after, nor above nor below, nor far nor near, nor union nor division, nor how nor where nor place. He is now as He was,

He is the One without oneness and the Single without singleness. . He is the very existence of the First and the very existence of the Last, and the very existence of the Outward and the very existence of the Inward. So that there is no first nor last nor outward nor inward except Him, without those becoming Him or His becoming them. He is not in a thing nor a thing in Him, whether entering in or proceeding forth. It is necessary that you know Him, after this fashion, not by learning (*'ilm*) nor by intellect, nor by understanding, nor by imagination, nor by sense, nor by the outward eye nor by the inward eye, nor by perception. By Himself He sees Himself and by Himself He knows Himself. . His veil, that is, phenomenal existence, is but the concealment of His existence in His oneness, without any attribute. . There is no other and there is no existence for any other, than He. . He whom you think to be other than God, he is not other than God, but you do not know Him and do not understand that you are seeing Him. He is still Ruler as well as ruled, and Creator as well as created. He is now as He was, as to His creative power and as to His sovereignty, not requiring a creature nor a subject. . When He called into being the things that are, He was already endowed with all His attributes and He is as He was then. In His oneness there is no difference between what is recent and what is original: the recent is the result of His manifestation of Himself and the original is the result of His remaining within Himself.

There is no existence save His existence. To this the Prophet pointed when he said: " Revile not the world, for God is the world," pointing to the fact that the existence of the world is God's existence without partner or like or equal. It is related that the Prophet declared that God said to Moses: "O My servant, I was sick and thou didst not visit Me: I asked help of thee and thou didst not give it to Me," and other like expressions. This means that the existence of the beggar is His existence and the existence of the sick is His existence. Now when this is admitted, it is acknowledged that this existence is His existence and that the existence of all created things, both accidents and substances, is His existence, and when the secret of one atom of the atoms is clear, the secret of all created things, both outward and inward, is clear, and you do not see in this world or the next, anything except God, for the existence of these two Abodesa nd their name, and what they name, all of them are assuredly He.

When the mystery—of realising that the mystic is one with the Divine—is revealed to you, you will understand that you are no other than God and that you have continued and will continue . . without when and without times. Then you will see all your actions to be His actions and all your attributes to be His attributes and your essence to be His essence, though you do not thereby become He or He you, in either the greatest or the least degree. "Everything is perishing save His Face," that is, there is nothing except His Face, "then, whithersoever you turn, there is the Face of God."

Just as he who dies the death of the body, loses all his attributes, both those worthy of praise and those worthy of condemnation alike, so in the spiritual death all attributes, both those worthy of praise and those to be condemned, come to an end, and in all the man's states what is Divine comes to take the place of what was mortal. Thus, instead of his own essence, there is the essence of God and in place of his own qualities, there are the attributes of God. He who knows himself sees his whole existence to be the Divine existence, but does not realise that any change has taken place in his own nature or qualities. For when you know yourself, your " I-ness " vanishes and you know that you and God are one and the same.

JALĀL AL-DĪN RŪMĪ (672/1273)

Jalāl al-Dīn Rumi was born at Balkh, but his family went to Konya in Rūm, hence his surname. He made a thorough study of Ṣūfism and devoted himself, in middle life, entirely to mysticism. He instituted the mystical dances, which were said to represent the revolution of the planets round their Sun, and were perhaps the beginning of the order of the Dancing Dervishes, who were known as " The Brethren of Love ", because the whole basis of their way of life was the love of God. The best-known of Rumi's works are " The Poems of Shams-i Tabrīz" (*Dīwān-i Shams-i Tabrīz*), a collection of beautiful lyrics, and " The Poem in Rhyming Couplets " (*Mathnawī*), a great mystical poem, which was said to have taken forty years to complete.

109

If the Divine Will seems to leave you in darkness, like the night, yet it will take your hand at the last : if the Divine Decree seems to threaten your life a hundred times, yet it is the Divine Decree that gives you life and a means of salvation.

It shines on every bough,
The blossom that the Spring has giv'n us now,
But soon is shed,
Its fruit can not appear, till it is dead.

The body, full of life,
Which gave itself to love and joy and strife,
Lies shattered :
And now the spirit can lift up its head.

Can bread give strength or feed,
Unless it first be broken for the need ?
Or shall the vine,
With grapes uncrushed, for others yield its wine ?

110

O hidden One, Who yet dost fill the world from East to West and art high above the light of the sun and moon. Thou Thyself art a mystery, yet Thou dost reveal our inmost secrets. Thou dost cause the rivers to flow forth, by Thy power. O Thou Whose Essence is hidden, while Thy gifts are manifest, Thou art like the water, while we are like the mill-stone : Thou art as the wind and we as the dust. The wind is concealed and the dust it produces is manifest to all. Thou art the Spring, we are like a garden fresh and fair : the spring is not seen, but its gifts are evident. Thou art as the spirit, we are as the hand and foot : the grasping and loosing of the hand are by the will of the spirit. Thou art like the reason, we like the tongue : the tongue takes its power to speak from the reason. Thou art as joy and we as laughter, for the result of joy is our laughter. All our actions are a profession of faith, for they bear witness to the glory of the Everlasting God.

111

O heart, why do you lie bound in this transient world ? Fly out from this cramped space, for you are a bird that belongs to the world of spirits. You are a friend that would always be alone, with the Beloved, abiding behind the veil of mystery. Why do you stay in this world, which is passing away ? Consider what state you are in, escape from your captivity in this material world and go forth to the grassy lawns of spiritual reality. You belong to the Divine world, you would be welcome in the assembly of Love : it would be grievous for you to remain in this abode. Each morning there comes a voice from heaven calling : " You will find the road clear for passage, when you make the dust to lie on it." On the way to the *Ka'ba* of union with Him, you will see at the root of every thorn, thousands who gave up their young lives for the sake of love. Thousands fell wounded on this road and there did not come to them any breath of the fragrance of union, or sign from the abode of the Beloved.

112

Why does the spirit not fly to its home, when the voice of the Divine Majesty is heard, with a fair message to the soul, saying : "Ascend" ? How should the fish not spring swiftly into the water, from the dry land, when it hears the sound of the waves from the limpid sea ? Why should a falcon not leave its prey and fly towards the King, when it hears the call to return, from drum and drum-strap ? Why, like a mote in the sunbeams, should not every Ṣūfī begin to shine forth in the sunshine of immortality that it may snatch him away from mortality ?

He gives such grace and excellence and beauty and newness of life, that he who turns aside from Him brings affliction on himself and is in error. Fly, fly onwards, O bird, towards the abode whence thou didst come, for thou hast gone forth from thy cage and thy wings are spread forth: make thy journey from the brackish water to the water of life. Return towards the spirit's home, from the place to which thou didst enter in. Go on thy way, O soul, for we also are coming from this world of separation to that world of union. Until when, like children, shall we fill our skirt with dust and stones and potsherds, in this earthly world? Let us leave the dust alone and let us fly towards the heavenly places. Let us leave childhood behind and seek the company of men.

113

Every form which you see has its original in the Divine world, where is no place. If the form passes away, it is of no consequence, since its original was from eternity. Be not grieved that every form which you see, every mystical saying which you have heard, has passed away, because that is not so. Since the fountain-head is abiding, its channel is always bringing forth water. Since neither ceases, why should you complain? Consider the spirit as a fountain and these creatures as rivers: while the fountain remains, the rivers flow from it. Put regret out of your thoughts and keep on drinking from the rivulet. Do not be afraid that the water will cease to flow: for this water is limitless.

From that time when you came into the world of created beings, a ladder was set before you, so that you might pass out of it. At first you were inanimate, then you became a plant: afterwards you were changed into an animal: why should this be hidden from you? At last you became man, possessed of knowledge, intelligence and faith. See how that body has become perfect, which was at first an atom from the dust-heap. When you have made your journey from man, without question you will become an angel. Then you will have finished with this world and your place will be in the heavens. Be changed also from the station of an angel: pass into that mighty deep: so that the one drop, which is yourself, may become a sea which would hold a hundred seas of 'Umān. Give up this polytheism of yours, say "God is One" with your whole heart and soul. If your body has become old, why grieve when your spirit is young?

114

By love bitter things are made sweet: copper turns to gold. By love, the sediment becomes clear: by love torment is removed. By love the dead is made to live: by love the sovereign is made a slave. This love also is the fruit of knowledge: when did folly sit on a throne like this?—The faith of love is separated from all religion: for lovers the faith and the religion is God..O spirit, in striving and seeking, become like running water: O reason, at all times be ready to give up mortality for the sake of immortality. Remember God always, that self may be forgotten, so that your self may be effaced in the One to Whom you pray, without care for who is praying, or the prayer.

115

Each moment the voice of Love is sounding from left and right; we are travelling on our way to heaven, who desires to look at anything on the way? At one time our home was in heaven, there we were in companionship with the angels. Let us go back to that abode, O Lord, for that is our dwelling-place. We are above the heavens and greater than the angels; why do we not go beyond these two? Our journey is to the vision of the glory of God. Whence is this earthly world, whence is the pure gem? Although we have descended thereto: let us hasten to return, for what place is this? The good fortune of youth is our means of strength: to surrender our lives is our business..The wave of "Am I not your Lord?" came and destroyed the vessel of the body: when the vessel is destroyed again, then is the opportunity for attaining union. Mortals, like water-birds, are born of the sea of spirit: why should a bird who has risen from that sea make his abode in this place? But we are pearls in this sea, all of us have our place in it: otherwise why should wave after wave come from the sea of spirit? It is the opportunity for us to attain union, the time to reach the beauty of immortality, the time to draw near and receive gifts, it is the ocean of perfect purity. The wave of gifts has appeared, the Throne of God has risen from the sea, the dawn of happiness has appeared: Is it the dawn? Nay, it is the light of God. God's light gives radiance to the light of sense: that is the meaning of Light upon Light. The light of the senses draws us towards the earth: the Light of God draws us up on high.

116

Each night Thou dost set the spirits free from the net of the body: Thou dost erase the tablets of memory. The spirits escape each night from this cage, set free from control and from speech and from the tales of men. At night prisoners are unaware of the prison, at night rulers forget their power. There is no anxiety, no thought of profit or loss, no consideration of this one or that. This is the state of the gnostic, even when awake. God said:

" They are asleep ", though they may seem to be awake. Be not afraid of this statement. He, that is, the gnostic, is asleep in regard to this world of affairs, both by day and night, like the pen which is moved by the hand of God. That one who does not see the hand, which is writing, thinks that the movement is due to the pen. A little of this state of the gnostic has been shown to us, since all creatures are subject to the sleep of the senses. Their souls have gone forth into the mysterious wastes: their spirits are at rest with their bodies. Thou callest them back into the net and bringest them all to justice and their judge. He Who created the dawn, like Isrāfīl, brings them all back from those spiritual regions into the material world..He has made the spirits to be like a horse free of its harness..this is the secret of " sleep is the brother of death ".

117

We were, once, one substance, like the Sun: flawless we were and pure as water is pure. Purify yourself, therefore from the qualities of self, so that you may see your essence, perfect and pure. If you seek for a parable of the knowledge which is hidden, hear the story of the Greeks and the Chinese.

The Chinese said: " We are the better artists ", and the Greeks rejoined: " We have more skill than you and more sense of beauty." So the king, in whose presence they were speaking, said to them: " I will test you in this, to see which of you is justified in your claim." —The Chinese then said: " Give us a room for ourselves and let there be a room for the Greeks." There were two rooms, with doors opposite each other: the Chinese took one room and the Greeks the other. The Chinese asked the king for a hundred different colours: the king opened his treasure-house for them to take what they would. Each morning the Chinese took from the treasure-house some of his gift of colours. But the Greeks said: "No colours or paints are needed for our work, which is only to remove the rust". They shut themselves in and polished continuously, until all was pure and clear like the sky. From many colours there is a way to freedom from colour: colour is like cloud and freedom from colour like the moon. Whatever radiance and light you see in the cloud, know that it comes from the stars and the moon and the sun.

When the Chinese had finished their work, they rejoiced and began to beat drums. The king came in and looked at the pictures which were there and when he saw them he was dumfounded. Then after that, he came to the Greeks: one of them raised the curtain that was between the rooms. The reflection of those paintings and the work the Chinese had done, fell upon those polished walls. All that the king had seen there, seemed more lovely here: the wonder of it made his eyes start from their sockets.

The Greeks are the Ṣūfīs, who dispense with study and books and learning, but they have purified their hearts, making them free from desire and greed and avarice and malice: that spotless mirror is undoubtedly the heart which receives images without number..Those who are purified have left behind them fragrance and colour: each moment they see Beauty without hindrance: they have left behind the form and the externals of knowledge, they have raised the standard of certainty. Thought has gone from them and they have found light, they have found the river and then the sea of gnosis..For the Ṣūfīs, there are a hundred signs from the Empyrean and the sphere above and the empty spaces, and what are these but the very Vision of God Himself?

118

O lovers, the time has come to depart from the world: the drum is sounding in the ear of my spirit, calling us to the journey. Behold, the camel-driver has bestirred himself and set his camels in their ranks and desires us to let him start. Why are you still sleeping, O travellers? These sounds which we hear from before and behind betoken travel, for they are the camel-bells. Each moment that passes, a soul is passing out of life and starting for the Divine world. From these gleaming stars and from these blue curtains of the heavens, have come forth a wondrous people, so that marvellous things of mystery may be made known. From these revolving orbs came a heavy sleep to you: beware of this so-transient life, have a care of this heavy sleep. O heart, depart towards the Beloved, O friend, go to your Friend. O watchman, keep awake, for sleep is not becoming to a watchman.

MAḤMŪD SHABISTARĪ (720/1320)

Maḥmūd Shabistarī spent most of his life at Tabrīz and lived at the time of the Moghul conquests of Persia, Syria and Irāq. His most famous work is "The Rose-Garden of Mystery" (*Gulshan-i-Rāz*), a long mystical poem which is one of the best accounts of Ṣūfism in existence. He also wrote other books on Ṣūfism.

119

Who is the traveller on the road to God? It is that one who is aware of his own origin. . He is the traveller who passes on speedily: he has become pure from self as flame from smoke. Go you, sweep out the dwelling-room of your heart, prepare it to be the abode and home of the Beloved: when you go out, He will come in. Within you, when you are free from self, He will show His Beauty ..When you and your real self become pure from all defilement, there remains no distinction among things, the known and the knower are all one.

But union with God is far from created things. To be His friend is to become a stranger to oneself. When it becomes possible for the contingent to pass away, nothing but the essential remains. Unity is like a sea..look and see how a drop from that ocean has found so many forms and has been given so many names, mist and water and rain and dew and clay, plant, animal and finally, man in his perfection. All come from one drop, at the last as at the first: from that drop all these things were fashioned..The phantoms pass away: in one moment there remains—in all places—only the Creative Truth. At that moment of time you come near to Him: parted from self, you can join the Beloved. In God there is no duality. In that Presence "I" and "we" and "you" do not exist. "I" and "you" and "we" and "He" become one..Since in the Unity there is no distinction, the Quest and the Way and the Seeker become one.

120

I have heard that, in the sea of 'Umān, the pearl-shells rise in the month of April. From the depths of the sea they come up and they rest on the surface of the sea, with open mouths. A mist rises from the sea and, by the command of the Almighty Lord, descends as rain: a few drops fall into each open mouth, which is then closed as by a thousand bands. The shell sinks to the bottom of the sea, with a full heart and each of those drops becomes a pearl. The diver plunges into the sea and from it brings forth an incomparable jewel. The Reason is the diver into this great sea, who has a thousand jewels wrapped in his blanket.

121

One, though in counting it be used of necessity, yet becomes no more than one by the counting. How can you doubt that this is like a dream: that beside Unity, duality is just a delusion? The differences that appear and the apparent multiplicity of things come from the chameleon of contingency. Since the existence of each of them is One, they bear witness to the Unity of the Creative Truth.

Everything which is manifest in this world is like a reflection from that world: it is like a curling lock and a beard and a mole and an eyebrow, for everything in its own place is good. The manifestation of the Divine Glory sometimes comes through Beauty and at another time through Majesty. The Divine world is infinite: how can finite words reach unto it? All these mysteries, which are known only by direct experience..how can they be explained by human speech? When the gnostics interpret these mysteries, it is by symbols that they are interpreted.

Wine and lamp and the beloved are symbols of the One Reality, Who in every form, is manifested in His glory. Wine and lamp are the light and the direct experience of the knower. Contemplate the Beloved, Who is hidden from no one. Drink for a while the wine of ecstasy: perhaps it may save you from the power of self. Yes, I tell you, drink this wine that it may save you from yourself and lead the essence of the drop into the ocean.

To become a haunter of taverns is to be set free from self: egotism is infidelity, even though one seem to be devout. The tavern belongs to the world beyond compare, the abode of lovers who fear nothing. The tavern is the place where the bird of the spirit makes its nest: the tavern is the sanctuary of God Himself.

122

The mystic who has seen the Vision of the Unity, sees at the first the light of Real Existence: even more, as he sees, by his gnosis, the pure light, in everything he sees, he sees God first. A condition for good reflection is solitude, for in that state a flash of the Divine Light brings us help. The essential has no likeness to the contingent. How can it be known by man? How foolish is he who seeks the radiant Sun by the light of a candle in a desert!

Not-being is the mirror of Being, that is, of Absolute Being. In it is reflected the glory of the Creative Truth. When not-being is placed opposite Being, in an instant the reflection appears in it. Not-being is a mirror and the world and the reflection and man are like the reflection of an eye..the eye of the Hidden One. Although the place which is the centre of the heart is small, it is yet found to be a fitting dwelling-place for the Lord of the Two Worlds.

Under the veil of each particle is concealed the soul-refreshing beauty of the Face of the Beloved. To that one whose spirit lives in contemplation of the Vision of God, the whole world is the book of God Most High.

123

The grace of the favour of the Lord Most High is forever being manifested in His work. On this side prosperity and perfection are seen, on that side every moment it is being changed. But when the state of this world passes away, all will be everlasting in the world to come. . Body and soul will appear as one unblemished substance. . you will contemplate the Creative Truth as He is, unveiled: by the light of the Creative Truth, you will be transfigured. When I have seen this Vision and have drunk from that wine, I know not what will come to pass for me henceforth.

SHAMS AL-DĪN ḤĀFIẒ (791/1389)

Ḥāfiẓ lived in Shīrāz, a famous poet, who was given the names of "The Tongue of the Unseen" (*Lisān al-Ghayb*) and "The Interpreter of Mysteries" (*Tarjumān al-Asrār*). In his later years he gave himself to the religious life and became a Ṣūfī shaykh. He passed much of his time alone, giving himself to the service of God and to meditation on the Divine nature. He collected his poems into a *Dīwān*, which became famous beyond his native land; many of his poems are mystical. He believed that God was revealed throughout nature and held that there was nothing which was not from God and a part of Him: the universe was His reflection upon the void of non-being.

124

The bird of my heart is a Divine bird which nests on the Throne of God. It has tired of the body's cage and become weary of life in this world. When the bird of the spirit flies from the top of this heap of dust—this world—it will find rest once more in that royal abode. When it takes its flight from this world, the lote-tree of Paradise will be its resting-place. Know that my falcon can rest only on the pinnacles of God's Throne..Its body is from the world below, but its spirit comes from the Divine world above, and is limited to no place. The world on high is my bird's fair dwelling-place: it drinks water in the gardens of Paradise.

125

None hath ever seen Thy Face, though thousands are looking in expectation of it. Thou art at rest in the rosebud and even now a thousand nightingales are seeking Thee. If I come by where Thou dwellest, it is not strange, since many are strangers wandering in that land. Far from Thee though I be—and pity it is that any should be far from Thee—nevertheless the hope of union with Thee is always near to me. To those who love Thee, there is no difference between monastery and tavern, for everywhere shines the light of the Face of the Beloved. Wherever glory is given to Thee in a place where Thou art worshipped, the bell which summons men to prayer, and the cloister and the monk and the name of the Cross, all serve one purpose. What lover of God is there whose state is not regarded by the Beloved? O sir, there is no pain for you in this, and if it should be otherwise, there is a Physician, Who can heal you.

126

My heart is the secret place where His love abides: my eyes hold the mirror to His Face. I, who have not bowed my head to either world, now bend my neck beneath the burden of His many favours. You desire the Tuba-tree in Paradise, I desire the presence of the Beloved—the thought of each one is according to his desire. If I, who desire to be in that sanctuary, where the zephyr holds the curtain which veils the shrine of His holiness, if I come with sin-stained garments, what does it matter, since the whole world is witness to His purity ? All that I have of the kingdom of a lover and all that I enjoy, I owe to His favour..May my eyes never be without the Vision of Him, for this secret place is the spot where He chooses to dwell apart with me. Every rose, as it opens its petals in the garden, has a colour and a perfume which is given to it, by Him.

Look not at the outward poverty of Ḥāfiẓ, for his inner self is the treasure-house of the Divine love.

127

It is an infamous thing to exalt oneself and to prefer oneself to all other creatures. You should learn a lesson from the pupil of the eye, which sees everyone else, and does not see itself.

O Lord, since Thou art He Who provides for all wants and Thou art both the Judge of what is needed and sufficient therefor, why should I tell the secrets of my heart to Thee, since all mysteries are laid open to Thee ?

128

O you who are without knowledge, make every effort to attain it. Until you have travelled over the road, how can you be a guide thereon ? In the school of Divine Truth, as you learn from the teachers of Love, strive in every way, my son, so that one day you may become a father in wisdom. Your concern with sleep and food have kept you far from the high station of Love. You will attain to the Beloved when you have learnt to do without sleep and food. If the radiance of the love of God falls on your heart and soul, surely you will become fairer than the sun in the firmament. Rid yourself of the copper of your own self, like the warriors of the Path, so that you may find the alchemy of Love and become gold. The light of God will shine on you, enveloping you from head to foot, when you are borne without head and foot along the Path of the All-Glorious. For one moment sink into the ocean of God, and do not suppose that one hair of your head shall be moistened by the water of the seven seas. If the vision you behold is the Face of God, there is no doubt that from this time forward you will see clearly. When the foundations of your own existence are destroyed, have no fear in your heart that you yourself will perish.

O Ḥāfiẓ, if in thine heart, thou dost crave for union, thou wilt need to become as the dust on the threshold of those who contemplate the Vision of God.

129

Nothing I behold, save the Vision of Thee: all paths I take are the road that leads to Thee. Though sleep falls gratefully upon the eyes of all, when Thou givest it, I pray Thee, O Lord, that my eyes may remain ever wakeful.

Where is the glad news of Union, that I may rise again? A holy bird am I, ascending from the vanities of this low world. If Thy love calls upon me to be Thy bondslave, I shall arise above the claims and the power of being and place. O Lord, give me the rain of guidance from

Thy clouds..O Beloved, towards Whom all men move and strive, from life in this world I will arise and live again in Thee.

'ABD AL-KARĪM JĪLĪ (832/1428)

'Abd al-Karīm Jīlī was a great Ṣūfī teacher who lived and taught in Baghdad, and appears to have been a member of the Qādiriyya order of dervishes. He was a prolific writer, who has left twenty mystical works and perhaps wrote others, and his doctrine was plainly the fruit of his own mystical experience. His best-known work is "The Man Perfect in Knowledge of the Last Things and the First" (*al-Insān al-kāmil fi Ma'rifat al-awākhir wa'l-awā'il*). His idea of Reality is Pure Thought, and his work had some influence upon the later religious development of Islām.

130

Thought is the basis of existence and the Essence which is in it, and it is a perfect manifestation of God, for Thought is the life of the spirit of the universe. It is the foundation of that life and its basis is Man. To him who knows Thought, who is given to know it by the power of the All-Great, existence is but a thought. Do not despise the power of Thought, for by it is realised the nature of the Supreme Reality.

When Pure being manifests itself in the world of Nature, names and attributes are attached to the Essence, and these really represent different points of view. They can be divided into four classes: there are those belonging to the Essence (*al-Dhāt*) and the highest of these are God, the One, the Eternal, the Real, the Creative Truth, the

Light. Then there are those belonging to the Divine Majesty (*al-Jalāl*), which give to God the name of the All-Glorious, the All-Powerful, the Exalted. Then there are names and attributes belonging to the Divine Beauty (*al-Jamāl*), such as the All-Merciful, the Omniscient, the Guiding Aright. The fourth class include those which belong to the Divine Perfection (*al-Kamāl*) which are the Creator, the First and the Last, the All-Wise, the Benefactor.

131

Existence is of two kinds, Absolute Existence, Pure Being, God as He is in Himself, unknowable, the " dark cloud " (*al-'Amā'*): and Existence joined with non-existence, that is, Nature as manifested in the universe. The Essence is One, but there are two forms of it, the Essence of the creatures and the Essence of the Creator.

The first stage of the descent of the Absolute towards manifestation is the stage of the Absolute Unity (*al-Aḥadiyya*) free from all attributes and relations, but yet no longer the pure undifferentiated Essence. It can be compared to a wall, which at a distance appears to be a whole, and the parts of which it is composed, cannot be distinguished, though it includes all those parts. Absolute Unity also is a unity which includes diversity.

The second stage of the descent is to the assertion of the Divine Individuality (*al-*Huwiyya), which shows the inner unity of all things, but not as yet any outward expression of that inner reality.

The third stage is that of the Divine Manifestation (*al-Aniyya*) which is the outward expression of that inner unity, revealed in existence, the One in the many. These two are reconciled in the stage of Simple Unity (*al-*

Wāḥidiyya), when the many are found to be identified in essence with each other and the One.

This unity is the outward manifestation of the Essence, which contains the attributes—that is, the different aspects of manifestation—as the attributes contain the Essence. When considered in this way, every attribute is the same as any other, and the first among them is one with God Himself, and He is one with the first of them.

I am the Existent and the non-existent :
That which comes to nought and that which abides.
I am that which is felt and that which is imagined :
I am both snake and charmer.
I am the loosed and the bound :
I am that which is drunk and he who gives to drink.
I am the treasure and I am poverty :
I am My creation and the Creator.

132

Man is the link between God and Nature. Every man is a copy of God in His perfection ; none is without the power to become a perfect man. It is the Holy Spirit which witnesses to man's innate perfection, the spirit is man's real nature and within him is the secret shrine of the Divine Spirit. As God has descended into man, so man must ascend to God, and in the Perfect Man —the true saint, the Absolute Being, which had descended from its Absoluteness, returns again unto itself.

In treading the Path, the Ṣūfī ascends until perfection is reached, and in the perfected saint, God and man become one again. .The original purity of the soul has become defiled by contact with this world and it must therefore be purified. Some are blest, in that they can purify themselves as easily as a garment that is slightly soiled can be washed clean in water, but some are so deeply stained that they can only be purified as by fire, by great self-discipline, renunciation of this world and the flesh, and by unceasing effort and struggle, including service to their fellow-men, who are also made in the image of God, and service to them is service to Him.

133

As the seeker proceeds, he has the sense of " Certainty ", the sign of Divine gnosis. The mystic knows, from the very first moment when he really begins to ascend on the upward way, that what is revealed to him is the light of God. The Divine illumination comes through meditation upon the names and acts the attributes and the Essence of God. The first stage is that of meditation upon the Divine acts, when man realises the power of God in the universe and knows that he himself has no power, but that all is done by the act of God. The second stage is that of meditation on the Divine names, when man knows himself to be of no account and the will of the individual is merged in the Divine Will. The third stage is that of meditation on the Divine Attributes, in which the mystic receives the attributes of God in place of his own, as he is able to receive them, and the Divine Spirit in place of the human spirit, and all that he does is done by that Spirit. It is no longer a case of " servant " and " Lord ", for only God remains. Now the mystic receives the final illumination, that of the Essence, the sphere of Absolute Existence, and has become the perfect Man. He is the one who has perfectly realised that he is one with the Divine Being in Whose image he was made, and he is now living the life of union with God. He sees through God, he hears through God, he speaks through God and he lives in God. So the return of the Divine Essence from manifestation to Absolutism is accomplished through the attainment of the unitive experience by the soul.

'ABD AL-RAḤMĀN JĀMĪ (898/1492)

Jāmī was born at Jām in Khurāsān, but spent most of his life at Herāt. While some gave him the name of "Lord of the Poets" and "Elephant of Wisdom", he chose to call himself the "The Ancient of Herāt". Jāmī avoided the society of patrons, but was famous as a poet during his lifetime. He devoted his whole life to study and writing and produced a biography of the Ṣūfī saints called "The Gifts of Fellowship" (N*afaḥāt al-Uns*) and a treaty on Ṣūfī theosophy "Flashes of Light" (*Lawā'iḥ*), as well as much fine mystical poetry.

134

O God, save us from the distraction of wanton pastimes and show us things in their reality. Take from our inner vision the veil of indifference and show us each thing as it really is. Do not let us see Not-Being in the form of Being and do not place the veil of Not-Being over the beauty of Being. Make this material world into a mirror for the manifestations of Thy loveliness, do not allow material things to be a means of concealment of Thy Presence and a means of keeping us far from Thee. Make these imaginary pictures to become the causes of knowledge and vision to us, let them not be a means of ignorance and blindness. Our loss of Thee and separation from Thee, all come from ourselves. Leave us not to ourselves, but save us from ourselves and grant to us knowledge of Thyself.

135

At the beginning of things, the Beloved unveiled His Beauty, in the solitude of the Invisible World. He placed before Himself the mirror of the invisible; He showed all His Beauty unto Himself, He was, in truth, both Seer and Seen: none except Him had looked upon this world. All was one, there was no duality: there was no assertion of "mine" or "thine". Though He saw the diversity of His attributes to be one and beautiful in His Essence; yet He desired they should manifest to Him in another mirror. It was seemly that every one of His eternal attributes should, after that, be displayed each in a different guise. So He created the life-giving meadows and the garden of the universe, so that, from every bough and flower and leaf therein, His Beauty should be manifested, in many different forms.

136

From that Divine Beauty light shone upon the rose and therewith the nightingale was filled with desire for the rose. From that light the candle was set aflame and everywhere a hundred moths were consumed by its fire. A single ray from its light made the sun ablaze and the lotus raised its head from the water. By that Divine Beauty the face of Layla was made fair and Majnūn was moved to love by every hair of hers. It was that which opened Shirīn's sweet lips and carried away the heart of Parvīz and the soul of Farhad. His Beauty is manifested in every place, and within those things in this world, which are counted fair, but are set behind a veil. Because of the Beloved, the moon of Canaan—Yūsuf—lifted up his head and Zulaykha, overcome with love, therewith became distraught. In every veil you see, the Divine Beauty is concealed, making every heart a slave to Him. In love to Him the heart finds its life; in desire for Him, the soul finds its happiness. The heart which loves a fair one here, though it knows it not, is really His lover.

Have a care, lest in error you speak idly, saying that from us is love and from Him is goodness. You are but the mirror, He is the picture reflected in the mirror; you are concealed, He is shown clearly; even if you receive praise for goodness and love, both come from Him and only appear in you. If you will look well, you will see that He is the mirror likewise, not alone the Treasure, but the Treasure-house also. If with discerning eye, you see everything to be good, if you look at that which you have found good, you will find it to be but the reflection of His Face. "I" and "Thou" are of no significance, except as figures of imagination; we have no right to interfere. Better be silent, for this tale has no end, there is none who can describe or interpret Him. It is better that we should be afflicted as lovers, for otherwise we are afflicted, being nothing.

Be the captive of Love in order that you may be truly free—free from coldness and the worship of self—Thousands who were wise and learned, who were strangers to love, have passed on their way. No name is left to them, nothing to proclaim their fame and dignity nor to relate their history in the march of time. Although you may attempt to do a hundred things in this world, only Love will give you release from the bondage of yourself.

137

O Thou, by Whom the souls of lovers are refreshed, by Whom new life is given to their tongues, upon the world has Thy protection fallen: all who are fair of face owe their fairness to Thee. All talk of beauty and of love comes from Thee and, in truth, both lover and beloved are of Thy making. Before Thee, the beauty of mortals is a veil, but Thou hast veiled Thy Face, and that Beauty is derived from itself. Thou hast veiled Thyself, as a bride is veiled, and none can see Thee or know Thee. When wilt Thou cease to torment us with this veil?

Once Thou didst withdraw this veil and wast revealed and now again Thou art showing Thy face and Thou dost bid us, as we look upon Thee, to pass away from self and to discriminate no more between what we think to be good or ill. As Thy lover, may Thy light be shed upon me so that I may see Thee in all things. Thou hast Thy place in all forms of truth and in the forms of created things there is none but Thou. Wheresoever I look, in all that I behold, throughout the world I see none but Thee.

138

It surely behoves you to make an effort and to turn away from self, and turn your face towards the Absolute Reality, and concern yourself with Him, Who is the Creative Truth. You must know that created things, in their different types, are all of them means whereby His Beauty is manifested, and the diverse classes of creatures are all mirrors which reflect His perfection. You must continue to strive in this way, until He dwells in your soul and your own existence passes out of your sight, and if you regard yourself, you are regarding Him, and when you say anything of yourself, you say it of Him.

That which was finite has become infinite and " I am the Truth " is the same as " He is the Truth ".

139

When God Most Glorious manifests His Essence to anyone, that one will find his own essence and his own attributes and his own actions to be utterly absorbed in the light of God's Essence and the Divine attributes and actions and will. He will see his essence to be the Essence of the One and his attributes to be the attributes of God and his action to be the actions of God, because of his complete absorption in union with the Divine; and beyond this stage, there is no further stage of union for man. For when the eye of the soul—the spiritual vision—is rapt away to the contemplation of the Divine Beauty, the light of understanding, whereby we distinguish between things, is extinguished in the dazzling light of the Eternal Essence and the distinction between the temporal and the eternal, the perishable and the imperishable, is taken away.

'ABD AL-WAHHĀB AL-SHA'RĀNĪ (AL-SHA'RĀWĪ)
(973/1565)

Sha'rānī was a late representative of Ṣūfism, an Egyptian, who lived a life of simple self-denial. He felt, and also expressed, great sympathy with the poor peasants of Egypt: in his time they were much oppressed by the Turks, who were then ruling over the country. Sha'rānī founded an order of Ṣūfīs called *al-Ṭarīqa al-Sha'rāwiyya*. He was a true mystic, laying great stress on the need for a personal experience of the life of fellowship with God. Most of his writings deal with mysticism, the best-known being a biography of the Ṣūfī saints, *Lawāqiḥ al-Anwār*, known as *al-Ṭabaqāt al-Kubrā* and also a work called " The Sacred Lights " (*al-Anwār al-Qudsiyya*).

140

When the servant has realised that all his actions proceed from his Lord and then he gives himself to meditation on any thing, how can his meditation profit him, for God is regarding his meditation, and indeed all things are under His regard ?..and a vision of his own shortcomings is more fitting for the servant, for then he can realise what true meditation means.

The end reached by the theologian, is the beginning of the way for the dervish, for the highest stage of the theologian is to be sincere in his knowledge and in what he does for the sake of God, and to show his sincerity in not seeking any reward for what he does ; he does not experience anything but this. But this is only the entrance to the Ṣūfī Path, for the seeker : from thence he ascends, according to the grace which is granted him and the part allotted to him. There are stages and states which he must attain all the time he is ascending, until he passes away from his consideration of all this and from himself, into the contemplation of the glory of his Lord.

141

The servant of God reaches the stage of giving himself to the service of his Lord, through acts of devotion, but only when he has ceased to think of his service, because he is preoccupied with his Lord and is contemplating Him at all times, has he reached true service to God because he is now under the Divine Will, and where else can he find rest ?

Then the servant passes on to the stage of steadfastness and realises that this also is a gift from God, Who enables him to be steadfast, and you must know that the result of steadfastness is that the servant ceases to claim or pray for anything, whether the thing which he seeks is his right or whether he has no right to it, whether it is an outward benefit or an inward gift.

Then the servant passes on to the stage of dependence upon God, for those servants of His, who are truly sincere, have come to know that God Most High has appointed all things to Himself and the servant has control over nothing, not even over his own property. He knows that God's judgment is All-wise and All-good.

The servant then passes to the stage of trust in God, and when His servants have reached this stage, they know that power belongs to God and they have no control over the matters which God has appointed to their care. So they are obedient to the command of their Lord, without consideration of why He desires anything, for they know that all He does is Wisdom itself.

142

The mystic seeks to be one of the people of gnosis concerning God, the gnosis which is the mark of the Ṣūfīs, but you must know that knowledge of God concerns His essential attributes (which keep Him apart from us), and His attributes manifested in action. If anyone asserts that he has knowledge of the attributes which belong to the Essence, which are eternal, his assertion is false, because it limits God to what can be conceived by the finite mind, and His Essence is without limit, infinite. There is a door which is closed to man, who is a creature, and it is not fitting that he should try to open it and concern himself with the Creative Truth.

The mystic also seeks to be one of those who are in fellowship with God, but it may be that to see himself in this light only shuts him out from the Presence of His Lord. For you must know that the servant is nearer to fellowship with God, when men shun him than when they accept him. Let the servant beware, lest he is deceived by the satisfaction he has in times of spiritual uplift. I say that delight in fellowship is the result of the grace accorded to the soul. The sincere servant is that one to whom fellowship and its absence are all the same ; how can that one have fellowship with the Creative Truth, who does not know Him, nor has any affinity with Him, nor intercourse with Him, who does not frequent His society and has never seen Him ? Fellowship can exist only with that one, with whom one is intimate, and intimacy is only with him with whom one has affinity and likeness and to whom one has drawn near, and this can be realised only by experience.

The mystic then seeks to be one of those who worships God, praising Him at all times and in all states, and it may be that to have this vision of himself is a hindrance. For that one who truly praises God Most High is unmindful of all else in His Presence. For all creatures, throughout the universe, glorify God, without weariness and to this, those possessed of revelation, bear witness. I myself have experienced this state from the time of the evening prayer until the first third of the night had passed, and I was listening to the things God has made, praising Him and lifting up their voices until I feared for my reason : then it was veiled from me by the mercy of God, as a favour, which I recognise..I heard the fish say: "Praise be to the King Most Holy, the Lord of riches and power and strength", and also the animals and the plants likewise, and in all their praises, I heard only this.

Then the mystic aspires to be one of those who merge their will in the Divine Will and this unity with God is not attained in truth except by detachment from all the creatures. For the idea of unity, which the servant has, is not free from defects, and unity with God must be thought of only in regard to Him, without a trace of anything beside Him.

143

The attributes of the saint are not known save to the saints, from where otherwise could they be known? For God exalts among His servants those who are faithful and not tempted by mankind: He perfects His light in their hearts and thereby establishes their inheritance from the prophets..How should the common people know the secrets revealed by God to the elect among His servants from among the saints and the wise, and the rising of His light in their hearts? Therefore He has made them to be veiled from mankind generally, because of their glory in His sight. For if what they possess were manifest and any man were to injure them, God would take action against such a one and destroy him, so their veiling by God from mankind, is an act of pity towards these others.

But the secret of saintship lies within and it is eternal ..Every saint has a veil or veils like the seventy veils with which the Ultimate Reality is veiled. Exalted is He and none but He knows the mystery behind the veils. So also it is with the saint.

144

The origin of the disputes of men with regard to the knowledge of Divine things and the signs of God, is the fact that these are beyond the scope of human minds and that these things come suddenly, without any warning or expectation, and not by way of the reason, and so men are ignorant of how they come. But the saint and the wise, in what they do, have sat in the company of God Most Glorious, acknowledging Him as the Truth, and have surrendered themselves wholeheartedly into His hands to do what He wills with them. They have given themselves to the contemplation of God the All-Glorious and have followed His guidance and cast themselves submissively into His hands. They have ceased to think of themselves, in humility before the Sovereignty of their Lord and are satisfied with His eternal rule over them. He does for them what they did formerly for themselves—the servant ceases to contemplate himself and gives himself up to the contemplation of his Lord.

FĀṬIMA JAHĀNĀRĀ BEGUM ṢĀḤIB (1092/1681)

Jahānārā was a typical representative of the Moguls and possessed of great ability. She early became interested in mysticism, was initiated into the order of the Qādiriyya dervishes and devoted herself to the study of Ṣūfism. When her father, the Emperor Shāhjahān was deposed and imprisoned by his son Aurangzeb, she shared his imprisonment, in order to minister to his needs. After his death, she was restored to all her dignities, but spent her time in devotion. She wrote an account of her mystical experiences in "The Treatise of the (Begum) Ṣāḥib" (*Risālat al-Ṣāḥibiyya*). She was called the "Rābi'a of the Age." (Cf. pp. 10 ff. above.)

145

I offer a thousand praises and thanks to God the Incomparable, for it was He Who, when my life was being spent to no purpose, led me to give myself to the great search for Him, and Who, after that, let me attain to the high degree of Union with Himself. He it was Who enabled me to quench my thirst in the ocean of Truth and the fountain of Gnosis and thereby granted me the unending happiness and state of blessedness, which are to be found by one who drinks from these. I pray that God Most High will let me walk in the Path which leads, like *Ṣirāṭ*, to Paradise, with firm step and unfaltering courage, and to taste the delight of continual recollection of Himself.

Praise be to God for His grace in what He has given to me. I have been granted full and perfect apprehension of the Divine Essence, as I had always most earnestly desired. That one who has not attained to knowledge of the Absolute Being is not worthy to be called a man —he belongs to the type of those of whom it is said: "They are like the beasts of the field and are even more ignorant". But he to whom this supreme happiness has been granted has become a perfect man and the most exalted of created beings, for his own existence has become merged in that of the Absolute Being. He has become a drop in the ocean, a mote in the rays of the sun, a part of the whole. In this state, he is raised above death and the fear of punishment, above any regard for Paradise or dread of Hell. Whether woman or man, such a one is the most perfect of human beings. This is the grace of God which He gives to whom He wills.

AḤMAD HĀTIF OF ISFAHĀN (1198/1784)

Hātif of Isfahān was a great Ṣūfī, who wrote in both Arabic and Persian. He was especially celebrated as a writer of *ghazals* and was the author of a famous poem of recurring lines (*tarjī'-band*). He writes as a lover of God and uses the imagery of the wine of the Divine Love which brings rapture and ecstasy to those who receive it.

146

To Thee we surrender both heart and life and cast down both this and that before Thee. The heart is surrendered to Thee, since Thou art the ravisher of hearts: life is given up to Thee, because Thou dost comprise all life. To release the heart from Thy hand is difficult: to give our life for Thy sake is not hard. The way to Union with Thee is a way that needs effort and means affliction: the anguish of love to Thee is a grief that cannot be assuaged. We are but bond-slaves, ready to give Thee our lives and our hearts, with an eye waiting for Thy command and an ear listening for Thy royal mandate. If Thine object is peace, our hearts are Thine and if Thy purpose be war, our lives are Thine to command.

147

Let the eye of your heart be opened that you may see the spirit and behold invisible things. If you set your face towards the region where Love reigns, you will see the whole universe laid out as a rose-garden. What you see, your heart will wish to have, and what your heart seeks to possess, that you will see. If you penetrate to the midst of each mote in the sunbeams, you will find a sun within, in the midst. Give all that you possess to Love and may I be considered an infidel if you find that you have suffered a barley-corn's worth of damage. If your spirit is dissolved in the flames of Love, you will see that Love is the Alchemy for spirit. You will journey beyond the narrow limitations of time and place and thence you will pass into the infinite spaces of the Divine World. What ear hath not heard, that you will hear, and what no eye hath seen, you shall behold: until you shall be brought to that high Abode, where you will see One only, out of the world and all worldly creatures. To that One you shall devote the love of both heart and soul, until with the eye that knows no doubt, you will see plainly that " One is and there is nothing save Him alone: there is no God save Him ".

148

From the shadow of door and wall the Beloved appears, unveiled, in all His Glory; O you who are possessed of insight, you are looking for a candle, while the sun is shining aloft: the day is radiant in all its splendour, while you remain in the depths of night. If you would only pass out from your own darkness, you would see the whole universe as the place where the dawn is breaking, where light begins to shine forth. As a blind man, you desire a leader and stick to help you along this road, which is quite smooth and level for your feet. Open your eyes to the Rose-garden and there you will see clear water shining within rose and thorn. From that clear water, without any colour of its own, come forth a hundred thousand different hues : you have only to look at the tulip and the rose in this fair flower-garden.

Set forth on the way to what you seek and take from Love what you need for travelling along this road : many things will become easy through Love, which beforetimes seemed to Reason very hard. Speak of the Beloved in the morning and at evening : look for the Beloved as night falls and as the day breaks. Though you are told a hundred times : " Thou shalt not see Me," yet continue to contemplate the Vision. You shall at last find the Beloved among His elect in a place, to which even Gabriel the faithful finds no admittance. This is the Way, this your provision, this is the Goal of the Quest.

QURRAT AL-'AYN CALLED ALSO JANĀB-I-ṬĀHIRA (1269/1852)

Qurrat al-'Ayn was a Bābī, well known for her poetry. She was included among the " Letters of the Living " (*Ḥurūfāt Ḥayy*), who made up the " First Unity " of the Bābī hierarchy ; she taught the Bābī doctrine at Kerbela and gained many converts to her faith. She was arrested and, refusing to recant, was put to death. Her poetry is definitely mystical.

149

Attraction to Thee and longing for Thee are fetters which have bound all Thine afflicted lovers with the chains of grief and sorrow : let them give their lives and surrender themselves in following Thee. If that One Whom I love, with seeming injustice, should seek my life, though I be innocent, I will surely rise up and give myself to His sword, and I will be satisfied with what pleases Him.

At the dawn that Beloved Who torments me, came to me as I lay sleeping, and when I looked upon His Beauty, it seemed to shine forth like the break of day. ..You who hold that wine and the Beloved are no concern of the devotee and ascetic..what shall I do, for like an infidel, you deny the holy faith and worship of the saints . Content with your desire for the dangling locks of a fair one, and for a horse and richly-dight saddle, you have throughout your life denied the Absolute One and have cared nothing for the poor and helpless. For you, the power and magnificence of Alexander, for me the custom and way of the wandering monk. If that be good, take it for yourself and if this is bad, it is proper for me. Leave the abode of " We " and " I " and choose as your country the kingdom of annihilation. For if you do this, you will truly attain to what you desire.

LIST OF SOURCES

1. Jāḥiz, *Bayān wa'l-Tabyīn* (Cairo A.H. 1332), III, pp. 68, 71 ; 'Aṭṭār, *Tadhkirat al-Awliyā* (London 1905), I, p. 40.
2. 'Aṭṭār, *op. cit.* I, p. 37 ; Abū Nu'aym, " Ḥilyat al-Awliyā " (MS. Damas), fol. 115.
3. Hujwīrī, *Kashf al-Maḥjūb* (Petrograd 1926), p. 274.
4. 'Aṭṭār, *Manṭiq al-Ṭayr* (Paris 1859), p. 143.
5. Aflākī, " Manāqib al-'Arifīn " (MS. India Office 1670), fol. 114a.
6. Jāmī, *Nafaḥāt al-Uns* (Calcutta 1859), p. 716 ; al-Makkī, *Qūt al-Qulūb* (Cairo A.H. 1310), II, p. 57 ; 'Aṭṭār, *Tadhkirat al-Awliyā*, I, pp. 69, 73.
7. Suhrawardī, *'Awārif al-Ma'ārif, Iḥyā* (Cairo A.H. 1272), IV, pp. 343, 358 (margin) ; al-Ḥurayfīsh, *al-Rawḍ al-Fa'iq* (Cairo A.H. 1300), p. 157.
8. Abū Nu'aym, " Ḥilyat al-Awliyā " (MS. Leyden), fols. 173b, 174a.
9. 'Aṭṭār, *Tadhkirat al-Awliyā*, II, pp. 3, 2.
10. *Ibid.*, I, pp. 1 ff.
11. " Waṣāya " (MS. Br. Mus. Or. 7900), fol. 26.
12. " Bad'man anāb ila Allah " (MS. Stambul Jarallah 1101), fol. 23b ; "Ādāb al-Nufūs " (ibid.), fol. 89b.
13. " Masā' il fi 'Amāl " (ibid.), fol. 123a ; " Fahm al-Ṣalāt " (ibid.), fol. 54b ; *Ri'āya* (London 1940), p. 28.
14. " Muḥāsabat al-Nufūs " (MS. Br. Mus. Or. 4026), fols. 66b, 67a ; " Kitāb al-Mustarshid " (MS. Cairo), fol. 2 ; "Ādāb al-Nufūs," fols. 101b ff.
15. " Bad' man anāb ila Allah," fol. 24a.
16. Abū Nu'aym, " Ḥilyat al-Awliyā " (MS. Leyden), fols. 231a ff., 238a, 232a.

17. Sarrāj, *Kitāb al-Lumac*, pp. 311, 313.
18. Jāmī, *Nafaḥāt al-Uns*, p. 26; 'Aṭṭār, *Tadhkirat al-Awliyā*, I, p. 127.
19. Sulamī, " Ṭabaqāt al-Ṣūfiyya " (MS. Br. Mus. Add. 18520), fols. 7, 8a.
20. 'Aṭṭār, *Tadhkirat al-Awliyā*, I, pp. 126, 127.
21. Khaṭīb, *Mishkāt al-Maṣābīḥ* (Lucknow A.H. 1319), VIII, pp. 394 ff.
22. 'Aṭṭār, *Tadhkirat al-Awliyā*, I, p. 310.
23. 'Aṭṭār, *Manṭiq al-Ṭayr* (Paris 1857), p. 86.
24. Sulamī, " Ṭabaqāt al-Ṣūfiyya," fol. 15a; 'Aṭṭār, *Tadhkirat al-Awliyā*, I, p. 157, 160.
25. *il-Qaṣd ila Allah* (Islamica 1926 II), pp. 404 ff.
26. Sarrāj, *op. cit.*, pp. 152 ff.
27. Sha'rānī, *Lawāqiḥ al-Anwār* (Cairo A.H. 1299), II, p. 79; Sarrāj, *op. cit.*, p. 33.
28. 'Aṭṭār, *Tadhkirat al-Awliyā*, II, pp. 54 ff.; Sarrāj, *op. cit.*, pp. 40, 59.
29. Hujwīrī *op. cit.*, pp. 399, 400; Sarrâj, *op. cit.* pp. 69, 300.
30. Ghazālī, *Iḥyā*, IV, p. 67.
31. Sarrāj, *op. cit.*, pp. 29–59.
32. M. b. al-Munnawar, *Asrār al-Tawḥīd* (Petrograd 1899), p. 378; Ghazālī, *Iḥyā*, IV, p. 288.
33. L. Massignon, *Quatres Textes* (Paris 1914), p. 78.*
34. Jāmī, *Bahāristān* (Vienna 1846), p. 7; Ghazālī, *Maqṣad al-Asnā* (Cairo), pp. 74, 75.
35. *Kitāb al-Mawāqif* (London 1935), p. 22.
36. *Ibid.*, p. 52.
37. *Ibid.*, p. 30.
38. *Ibid.*, p. 103.
39. *Rasā'il* (Cairo 1928), III, p. 275.
40. *Ibid.*, III, p. 318.
41. *Kitāb al-Luma'*, p. 46.
42. *Ibid.*, p. 154.
43. *Ibid.*, pp. 41, 213.
44. *Kitāb al-Ta'arruf* (Cairo 1934), p. 81.
45. *Ibid.*, pp. 80, 78.

46. *Qūt al-Qulūb*, I, pp. 199, 248 ff., 270 ff., II, p. 53, I, pp. 133, 119, 135, 151.
47. *Ibid.*, I, pp. 8, 6.
48. *Traités Mystiques* (Leyden 1879–1889), *Risālat Ḥayy b. Yaqẓān*, p. 21; *Māhīyat al-Ṣalāt* (Cairo 1917), pp. 37, 39.
49. *Traités Mystiques, Fi'l-'Ishq*, pp. 2 ff.; *al-Ishārāt wa'l-Tanbīhāt* (Leyden 1892), *Fī maqāmāt al-'Arifīn*, pp. 202 ff.
50. *Die Rubā'is des Abū Sa'īd* (ed. Ethé 1875), No. 41; M. b. al-Munawwar, *op. cit.*, p. 259.
51. M. b. al-Munnawwar, *op. cit.*, pp. 383, 384.
52. *Ibid.*, pp. 388, 389, 371.
53. *Ibid.*, p. 399.
54. Ethé, Nos. 82, 30.
55. *Ibid.*, Nos. 22, 38, 41.
56. *Ibid.*, Nos. 27, 17, 54.
57. *Risāla* (Cairo 1867), pp. 106, 82, 53, 177.
58. *Kashf al-Maḥjūb*, pp. 9, 424.
59. *Ibid.*, pp. 220, 452.
60. *Ibid.*, pp. 370, 402.
61. *Ibid.*, pp. 347, 351.
62. *Ibid.*, pp. 490, 492, 312.
63. *Iḥyā*, IV, p. 275, I, pp. 79 ff.
64. *Ibid.*, I, pp. 129, 130; *Bidāyat al-Hidāya* (Cairo A.H. 1349), p. 39.
65. *Kīmiyā al-Sa'āda* (Cairo A.H. 1343), pp. 4, 5.
66. *Ayyuha'l-Walad* (Cairo A.H. 1349), pp. 40, 46; *Rawḍat al-Ṭālibīn* (Cairo A.H. 1344), p. 143.
67. M. al-Murtaḍa, *Itḥāf al-Sa'āda* (Cairo A.H. 1311), p. 24.
68. *Iḥyā*, IV, p. 187.
69. *Ibid.*, II, pp. 246, 247.
70. *Mishkāt al-Anwār* (Cairo A.H. 1343), pp. 108, 109; *Kīmiyā al-Sa'āda*, p. 16; *Iḥyā*, III, pp. 18, 19.
71. *Ibid.*, IV, pp. 256, 262 ff. II, p. 247.
72. *Ibid.*, IV, pp. 269, 267.
73. *Kitāb al-Arba'īn* (Cairo A.H. 1344), pp. 52 ff. 55.

74. *Mishkāt al-Anwār*, pp. 118, 144, 145.
75. *Iḥyā*, IV, pp. 84, 286 ; *Mizān al-'Amal* (Cairo A.H. 1342), p. 107.
76. *Iḥyā*, IV, p. 252, II, pp. 236, 237.
77. *Ḥadīqat al-Ḥaqīqa* (Per. Bib. Indica 1911), pp. 6, 25, 37, 2, 7.
78. *Ibid.*, pp. 10, 57, 59.
79. *Ibid.*, pp. 7, 8.
80. *Ibid.*, pp. 82, 42, 43, 16.
81. al-*Munāwī*, " al-Kawākib al-Durrīya " (MS. Brit. Mus. Ad. 23, 369), fol. 51b.
82. *Futūḥ al-Ghayb*, M. al-Tādifī, *Qalā'id al-Jawāhir* (Cairo A.H. 1303), pp. 12 ff. 121 (margin).
83. L. Massignon, *Textes Inédits*, p. 111.
84. " Ḥikmat al-Ishrāq " (MS. Brit. Mus. Ar. Or. 36), fol. 5b, 5a.
85. *Manṭiq al-Ṭayr*, (Paris 1857) p. 103.
86. *Ibid.*, p. 45.
87. *Ibid.*, p. 90.
88. *Ibid.*, p. 157.
89. *Pandnāma* (Paris 1819), pp. 27 ff.
90. *Manṭiq al-Ṭayr*, p. 45.
91. *Jawhar al-Dhāt*, *Kulliyāt* (Teheran A.H. 1289), p. 23.
92. *Manṭiq al-Ṭayr*, p. 137.
93. *Pandnāma*, pp. 83 ff.
94. *Jawhar al-Dhāt*, *Kulliyāt*, p. 5.
95. *Mukhtār*, *Kulliyāt*, p. 969.
96. *Jawhar al-Dhat*, pp. 15, 16.
97. *Bīsār Nāma*, *Kulliyāt*, p. 1225.
98. *'Awārif al-Ma'ārif*, *Iḥyā* II (margin), pp. 292, 305 ff. p. 6.
99. *Ibid.*, p. 12.
100. *Ibid.*, pp. 223 ff. 232.
101. *Ibid.*, III, pp. 218, 219.
102. *Ibid.*, IV, pp. 407, 367, 369.
103. *Dīwān* (Marseilles 1853), pp. 347, 250, 252.
104. *Tā'iyya* (Vienna 1854), lines 680 ff., 702 ff.

105. *Dīwān*, pp. 257, 260.
106. *Tarjumān al-Ashwāq* (London 1911), p. 19.
107. *al-Futūḥāt al-Makkiyya* (Cairo A.H. 1293), III, p. 365.
108. *Kitāb al-Ajwiba* (J.R.A.S. 1901), pp. 810, 813, 817, 815, 816.
109. *Mathnawī* I (London 1925), pp. 78, 180.
110. *Mathnawī* V (London 1933), pp. 210 ff.
111. *Dīwāni Shamsi Tabrīz* (Cambridge 1898), p. 174.
112. *Dīwān*, p. 116.
113. *Ibid.*, p. 46.
114. *Mathnawī*, pp. 330, 343; *Dīwān*, p. 16.
115. *Dīwān*, pp. 32, 34; *Mathnawī*, II, p. 317.
116. *Mathnawī*, pp. 25 ff.
117. *Mathnawī*, I, p. 43, pp. 213 ff., II, p. 252.
118. *Dīwān*, p. 140.
119. *Gulshan-i Rāz* (London 1880), p. 19, pp. 24 ff. pp. 28 ff. p. 27.
120. *Ibid.*, p. 34.
121. *Ibid.*, pp. 42, 47, 49.
122. *Ibid.*, pp. 6, 9, 13.
123. *Ibid.*, pp. 40 ff.
124. *Dīwān* (Calcutta 1881), p. 164.
125. *Ibid.*, p. 28.
126. *Ibid.*, p. 8.
127. *Ibid.*, pp. 217, 219.
128. *Ibid.*, p. 181.
129. *Ibid.*, p. 156.
130. *al-Insān al-Kāmil* (Cairo 1886), II, p. 26.
131. *Ibid.*, I, 14, 47, 29, 7.
132. *Ibid.*, II, p. 46, I, pp. 9, 15 ff.
133. *Ibid.*, I, pp. 5, 37 ff. 41, 47 ff. 17 ff.
134. *Lawā'iḥ* (London 1928), p. 2.
135. *Tuḥfat al-Aḥrār* (London 1848), p. 36.
136. *Yūsuf u Zulaykha* (Lucknow 1880), pp. 22 ff.
137. *Salāmān u Absāl* (London 1850), p. 1.
138. *Lawā'iḥ*, p. 10.
139. *Nafaḥāt al-Uns*, p. 527.

140. *Anwār al-Qudsiyya*, *Lawāqiḥ al-Anwār* (Cairo A.H. 1299), II, pp. 128, (margin).
141. *Anwār al-Qudsiyya*, II, pp. 129, 133 ff. 137.
142. *Anwār al-Qudsiyya*, II, pp. 152, 156 ff. 163.
143. *Lawāqiḥ al-Anwār*, I, pp. 6 ff.
144. *Ibid.*, I, p. 9.
145. Tawakkul Beg Kulālī, " Neskhah-i-Aḥwāl Shāhī " (MS. Brit. Mus. Or. 3203), fols. 42a ff.
146. Luṭf 'Ali Beg, *Atash-kada* (Bombay A.H. 1277), *Tarji'band*, p. 417.
147. *Ibid.*, p. 418.
148. *Ibid.*, p. 418.
149. J. Royal As. Soc., 1899, pp. 936 ff., 991; E. G. Browne, *The Bābī Religion*, p. 359.

INDEX

Titles of books and Arabic and Persian words are printed in italics.